20.00

Raven: A Journal of Vexillology
© 2018 North American Vexillological Association
Post Office Box 55071 #58049
Boston, MA 02205-5071 USA
www.nava.org

ISBN: 978-0-9747728-7-5
ISSN: 1071-0043
Printed in USA

RAVEN

a journal of vexillology

VATICAN FLAGS

KEYS & CROWNS SINCE 1800

William M. Becker

*The flags of the Papal States
and today's Vatican*

North American Vexillological Association
Volume 25 – 2018

Figure 0.1. St. Peter's Basilica & the Vatican Flag, Residenza Paulo VI, 2005 (Extraterritorial Zone)

RAVEN

Volume 25 — 2018

CONTENTS

VATICAN FLAGS

3. Vatican City (1870–Today)

About the Association

Founded in 1967, the North American Vexillological Association (NAVA) is a United States-Canadian binational non-profit organization dedicated to vexillology, the study of flags and their cultural, historical, political, and social significance. It is the largest association of its kind in the world. NAVA recognizes and promotes excellence in vexillological scholarship through its publications program, annual meetings, and flag-conservation and flag research grant programs. NAVA serves flag collectors and historians, educators, museum professionals, government officials, flag manufacturers and retailers, writers, designers, and those interested in flags as a hobby.

À propos de l'Association

Fondée en 1967, l'Association nord-américaine de vexillologie (NAVA) est une organisation binationale canado-américaine sans but lucratif qui se consacre à la vexillologie, c'est-à-dire l'étude des drapeaux et leur importance culturelle, historique, politique, et sociale. Il s'agit de la plus grande association du genre au monde. NAVA reconnaît et promeut l'excellence dans les études vexillologiques par le biais de son programme de publications, de ses réunions annuelles, et de ses programmes de subventions pour la recherche sur les drapeaux ou leur conservation. NAVA dessert les collectionneurs et les historiens, les éducateurs, les professionnels oeuvrant dans les musées, les représentants gouvernementaux, les fabricants et les détaillants de drapeaux, les écrivains, les concepteurs, et les amateurs passionnés de drapeaux.

For membership information, contact

> NAVA
> attn.: Membership Committee
> Post Office Box 55071 #58049
> Boston, MA 02205-5071, USA
>
> e-mail to membership@nava.org, or visit www.nava.org

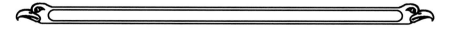

About Raven

Raven: A Journal of Vexillology is the peer-reviewed annual journal of academic vexillological research published by NAVA since 1994. It usually publishes 4–5 articles per issue; special issues such as this one have appeared as books (on flags of Native American tribes, U.S. cities, Canadian cities, and Russian regions). Articles appearing in *Raven* are abstracted and indexed in *Historical Abstracts* and *America: History and Life*. Information concerning permission to reprint articles is available from the *Raven* editor. Material appearing in *Raven* does not necessarily reflect the policy or opinion of NAVA, the NAVA executive board, its publication committee, or the Raven editor.

Subscriptions: Free to NAVA members, US$40 per year for non-NAVA members (includes a subscription to the quarterly *Vexillum*). Membership information is available by contacting the NAVA membership committee. Back issues are available at www.nava.org/raven.

Submission of Articles: For guidelines and schedule, contact the *Raven* editor, c/o NAVA, or by e-mail to raven@nava.org. Send articles to the *Raven* editor in electronic form in Microsoft Word, with a minimum of formatting and with images included as separate files. Do not use the footnote/endnote function. Articles are subject to an annual juried review and accepted based on criteria set by the Editorial Board. Authors of accepted articles must sign a publication agreement assigning copyright to NAVA and affirming that the material is original and not previously published elsewhere. Articles will be edited for style, consistency, and length.

Figure 0.2. Vatican flag, Apostolic Palace, Cortile di San Damaso, 2017

Donors

NAVA thanks the generous supporters whose financial contributions made this book possible.

Ernest E. Aitchison, Esqr.

Stratis Andreadis

STOLLENWERK
FAMILY FOUNDATION

Rev. William M. Becker

The Family of Whitney Smith, Jr.

Peter Ansoff	Art Etchells	David F. Phillips
Keith Bassolino	Mike Gahan	Gary Picou
William Belanich, Jr.	Lee Herold	Gavin Rehkemper
Alan Cooper	Edward B. Kaye	Rev. Michael B. Smith
CRW Flags	Ron Lancaster	Elijah Snow-Rackley
Charles Daschbach	John A. Lowe	Ron Strachan
Peter Edwards	R. Blaine Miller	Anonymous

Figure 0.3. Swiss Guard Barracks, 2007

Figure 0.4. Gendarmerie Headquarters, 2010

Foreword

George Weigel

 Human beings are endlessly inventive, and two of our most inventive inventions are postage stamps and flags. How does it happen that a small, gummed piece of colored paper gets a letter or parcel from one place to another? That seems odd, if you step back and think about it. Even more curiously, how is it that an often-multicolored cloth, usually attached to a pole, evokes sentiments of loyalty and courage, or, conversely, odium and fear?

The flags that Father William Becker explains in this marvelous book are especially interesting because they represent one of the world's oldest and yet least understood institutions: the papacy. And as Father Becker takes us through the history of the flags that have been used by popes and institutions affiliated with the papacy (like the Swiss Guard), he offers us a succinct summary of the remarkable modern story of this institution, which has changed dramatically over the past two hundred years.

The first flags in this book date from the years when popes were sovereign rulers of a large swath of Italy known as the Papal States—absolute monarchs who governed largely through clergymen who acted as civil as well as religious authorities. Then the Papal States slowly shrank under the pressures of the drive to unify Italy. After that process was completed by the conquest of Rome and its establishment, by force of arms, as the new Italy's capital, the popes retired behind the Leonine Wall surrounding St. Peter's Basilica and the buildings usually known as "the Vatican." They no longer controlled any territory, but there were still papal flags, for even without territory the popes continued to exercise what many nations recognized as "sovereignty". Why?

Because the pope, as Bishop of Rome, remained the embodiment of what was, then and now, known as "the Holy See": a unique entity, with no parallel in the world, recognized in international law and diplomatic practice as the sovereign expression of the pope's role as universal pastor of the Catholic

Figure 0.5. Palazzo del Governatorato, 2007

Church. Whether the pope controlled territory or not, the Holy See remained, in the language of international law and diplomacy, a "juridical personality". Thus popes exchanged ambassadors and other forms of diplomatic representation with various countries, even when the pope effectively controlled nothing but the house he lived in, the great basilica named for the first pontiff, and a number of buildings adjacent to St. Peter's and to the apostolic palace.

That situation changed, and the popes recovered a measure of control over a small territory, with the 1929 Lateran Accords, a set of agreements between the Holy See and the Kingdom of Italy. Those treaties recognized the existence of Vatican City State: a contiguous 108-acre territory around St. Peter's (plus some non-contiguous, "extraterritorial" properties in Rome and its environs) under papal sovereignty—and the flag of the new state was carefully prescribed in its constitution. This history can seem a minor footnote to the great contests for power that have characterized the modern world. But the endurance of the Holy See, and the capacity of the pope to act internationally without the political interference of another sovereign power, are important for the world as well as the Catholic Church. The tendency of political modernity is to subsume everything within the state. The papal flag reminds us that there is more to the world, even the political world, than states.

Popes no longer wield any real temporal power and Vatican City State is not a significant actor on the world stage. But the papacy is. Under John Paul II, who was pope from 1978 until 2005, the pope and the Holy See exercised greater leverage in world affairs than at perhaps any point since the High Middle Ages—and certainly more authority than at any previous moment in modern history. Thus the papal flag, today, reminds the world that moral truth and conviction continue to play an important role in human affairs. The course of history can be bent in a more humane direction by the power of moral argument and moral witness: that's what the yellow-and-white banner with the keys given by Christ to St. Peter proclaims.

Flag lovers will be intrigued by the story that Father Becker tells and by the striking images in this book. But *Vatican Flags* is not for flag lovers alone. The story it tells is full of important reminders that there are different forms of power in the world, and that the human condition cannot be reduced to politics alone, or economics alone, or some combination of politics-and-economics alone. The realm of the spirit still counts, and soulcraft shapes the future at least as much as statecraft.

George Weigel *is Distinguished Senior Fellow of the Ethics and Public Policy Center in Washington, D.C., where he holds the William E. Simon Chair in Catholic Studies.*

Figure 0.6. Benedict XVI and Vatican flag, Apostolic Palace, Cortile di San Damaso, 2007

Preface

 Since boyhood I have loved flags. I recall admiring the shapes and colors of the world's banners in our home encyclopedia. Among them was the yellow-white flag of Vatican City, bearing the crossed keys and tiara.

I remember, too, when I finally associated that flag with the one displayed in our parish church. My pastor called it "the papal flag", which confused me, until I learned that the pope lives at the Vatican. He also explained the flag's emblem: the pope holds the keys of St. Peter, who received them from Jesus Christ: "I will give you the keys of the kingdom of heaven" (Matthew 16:19). Other things he couldn't explain. Why was the flag square in books, but not in our sanctuary? Why were the yellow shades different? Why are the pope's colors yellow and white?

Later I lived in Rome as a seminarian and priest. For eight years I saw the Vatican flag up close, and studied its Papal States progenitors. I learned that not until the past century did the term "papal flag" imply a uniform design, for in the Papal States, flags varied. For over 30 years my ongoing research was published in installments—and finally, in this book. Here then, is a systematic record of the pope's legacy in the world of flags—today's chief symbol of sovereignty. It is especially fitting as the Holy See and Italy observe the 90th anniversary of the Lateran Accords, which established Vatican City's statehood in 1929.

As always, gratitude is in order. First, I thank the late Dr. Whitney Smith, who directed the Flag Research Center in suburban Boston. For many years he edited the *Flag Bulletin*, a journal which hosted several of my forays into this topic; and he was an invaluable contributor to my research. A true scholar and gentleman, he introduced me to vexillology—the study of flags. (The

Figure 0.7. John Paul II draped in a papal banner, Colombia, 1986

Figure 0.8. Vatican flag flying above the Vatican Museums, 2004

Whitney Smith Flag Research Center Collection is now housed at the University of Texas at Austin.) I likewise thank the North American Vexillological Association (NAVA) for supporting and publishing this work, as well as Ted Kaye, George Weigel, Scott Mainwaring, Steve Knowlton, Jeannie Galick, Kent McDaniel, and Francisco Gregoric for their expert contributions to the project. I am both humbled and honored.

I also thank various museums, especially the Museo Storico Vaticano, the Royal Museum of the Army in Brussels, and the Musée de la Civilisation in Québec City; several Roman libraries, especially the Istituto per la Storia del Risorgimento Italiano, and the Biblioteca Casanatense; the Vatican Secret Archives and Swiss Guard archives; Google Books; and a number of Italian devotees of Papal States history, especially Prince Sforza Ruspoli. For all of this able assistance, as well as the scholars listed in my bibliography, I am grateful.

The English writer G. K. Chesterton once marveled at a papal flag flying at a remote Irish farm, fêting it as "a tower of crowns and a parade of keys". It serves the world's smallest nation-state, but it also represents a global church; hence, paradoxically, the Vatican flag is among the most widely flown on the planet. To it, I offer this tribute—and to the shepherd who carries its keys: *ad moltos annos vivas!*

Figure 0.9. The Bishop of Winona-Rochester delivers Rev. Becker's flag research to John Paul II, 2004

Figure 0.10. Palazzo delle Congregazioni ai Propilei, 2017 (Extraterritorial Zone)

Prologue

The Lateran Treaty

This book happily anticipates the 90th anniversary in 2019 of the threefold Lateran Accords (1929). Among these, the "Lateran Treaty" affirmed the sovereignty of both the Holy See and Italy, established Vatican City State, and renounced papal claims to the millennium-old Papal States. A Concordat also regularized Roman Catholicism within Italy, and a Financial Convention compensated the pope for the loss of his old lands.

Among these accords, the Lateran Treaty interests us here. It has succeeded beyond expectations, in resolving the "Roman Question" that bedeviled diplomats well before the creation of the Kingdom of Italy in 1861, or its seizure of papal Rome in 1870. Among the Treaty's accomplishments has been the creation of a new "Papal State" with flexible borders and willing inhabitants, who now fly the papal flag proudly.

This "flexible" territory is due not only to Vatican City itself, but even more, to the 17 zones of the Holy See that currently enjoy full extraterritorial immunity under the Treaty, and successive agreements based upon it. These zones augment the papal state, and host shrines, offices, and educational and religious institutes throughout Rome and its environs. Several zones are in the Vatican area, and others beyond it; but when combined with Vatican City's 108 acres, the Holy See's civil jurisdiction comprises about 2 square miles in total. (Curiously, that tempers the Vatican's honor as the world's smallest nation-state, for its civil jurisdiction is actually larger than Monaco's; and additional sites are immune from Italian seizure.)

The borders of this enlarged papal state are also highly adaptable, because new zones are typically established or suppressed through a simple diplomatic "exchange of notes" with Italy, rather than concluding a full-fledged treaty

Figure 0.11. Residenza Paolo VI, 2017 (Extraterritorial Zone)

Figure 0.12. Palazzo dei Convertendi, 2018 (Extraterritorial Zone)

(though at times, that is done). Comparable arrangements elsewhere in the world don't exist—especially since the zones flex when needed, exceed Vatican City's area by roughly twelve times, and fly its flag more widely.

The outcome is not without its ironies. Today most of the extended Vatican area is owned by the Holy See (and is often extraterritorial), or is lodged by diplomats accredited to it, or is reliant on it for tourism and commerce; and the entire area has become the heart of the augmented papal state. But in 1870, neither the residents of the district nor the pope himself would settle for such an arrangement.

That year, about to seize Rome and the surrounding Lazio region, Italy proposed that the pope accept a reduced state in the Vatican area called the "Leonine City". This comprised the Vatican and Borgo area within the Leonine walls, on the west side of the Tiber River, opposite Rome proper to the east. (The name gave birth to the smaller "Vatican City" in 1929.) Pius IX declined, stating that even if the then-Italian government wanted to keep its word, it might not be able to do so. History must unfold first.

That is, a democratic Italy might one day reverse course, and seize the microstate too; and indeed, Italy was about to break its promise not to attack Rome in the first place. Still, when Italy's army seized Rome on 20 September 1870, the Leonine City was left inviolate, to preserve the prospect of papal rule there. The pope insisted that Italy occupy it due to likely protests by its residents against continued papal rule. Once occupied, the papal flag was lowered over the adjacent fortress, Castel Sant'Angelo, on 21 September. (Ironically, the son of the fort's commander would write the official flag study in 1929 which recommended the current Vatican flag design.)

After Pius declined the offer, Italy provided lesser guarantees based on an earlier concept. The latter suggested the pope's own person be regarded as sovereign, but without sovereign territory. Whatever building he inhabited would then become extraterritorial by virtue of his presence. (The problems inherent in such a "roving" sovereignty are apparent; but the notion is echoed in current provisions that, whenever the Sovereign Pontiff assists ceremonies at any Italian church, it becomes extraterritorial for the occasion.)

This concept of personal sovereignty laid the basis for the Law of Guarantees enacted by Italy in 1871. That law accorded the pope a sovereign's honors (but not the actual status), and treated his immediate residence with rights akin

Figure 0.13. Italy's Quirinal Palace, Papal Visit, 2008 (Former papal residence; current presidential residence)

to extraterritorial immunity. The result was not permanent; but in retrospect it seems a germ of the Lateran Treaty's distinction between today's sovereign microstate and those external zones governed by it.

In hindsight, conflicts over papal sovereignty were partly due to the shifting paradigm of sovereignty itself. For roughly a millennium, "sovereignty" implied a divine right to rule, as enshrined in noble lineage; and the Church itself was understood as a sovereign entity, headed by the pope. His right to rule it was found in divine scripture, and his See was often held or surrounded by an array of nobles among the bishops, cardinals, lower clergy, and others.

That all underwent a violent watershed during the French Revolution. The bloody events that ensued convulsed Europe; and only in time would sovereignty be reconceived globally, as the "popular will," enshrined in a territorial state. Once that new paradigm held sway, the pope's inherent sovereignty demanded territory, even a nominal amount. But it first required Italy to acknowledge the Holy See as sovereign by nature, and not by mere beneficence, whether Italian or international—though both are also key.

Whether papal sovereignty is rooted in divine or civil law—as was sometimes debated—is hardly the point. It is simply self-evident, because no civil leader of sound mind could pretend to govern the spiritual leader of a global Church with (currently) over a billion souls (just as no pope could again expect to rule a large state). Once Italy accepted the principle of "inherent" papal sovereignty, and the pope was ready to accept a microstate, the groundwork was laid for a solution; and the Lateran Treaty could be born.

All this shows that in the search for peace anywhere, ideas that seem less credible in one era, often bear fruit in another. In this light, one wonders whether the successful sharing of Rome between Italy and the Pope—negotiated after 70 years of acrimony between the two sides—could be a model of sorts for other conflicted lands. (The potential future sharing of Jerusalem comes to mind; exchanges of sovereignty and/or extraterritoriality between Israel and Palestine have been proposed there, too.)

Indeed, just as Vatican and Italian flags now fly alongside each other throughout Rome in amity and goodwill—a display once unthinkable—perhaps other flags might one day do the same. To that end, may leaders of goodwill flourish and prevail; and may the Bishop of Rome and his yellow-white banner help to inspire their cause.

Figure 0.14. Francis and Vatican flag, White House, Washington, D.C., 2015

Notes on Illustrations

Illustration acknowledgments for introductory pages follow. Subsequent acknowledgments are detailed in chapter endnotes and in Illustration Credits.

0.1 – AP Photo/Claudia Gazzini, 18 April 2005, licensed via: <www.apimages. com/metadata/Index/Associated-Press-International-News-Italy-Vatic-/3d54a1701 9e1da11af9f0014c2589dfb/241/0>.

0.2 – Andrea Franceschini/Pacific Press, 6 May 2017, licensed via: <www.alamy. com/stock-photo-swiss-guards-attend-a-swearing-in-ceremony-in-vatican-city-on- may-140021579.html>.

0.3 – *L'Osservatore Romano*, 6 May 2009, licensed by author.

0.4 – *L'Osservatore Romano*, 10 May 2010, licensed by author.

0.5 – *L'Osservatore Romano*, 31 May 2007, licensed by author.

0.6 – *L'Osservatore Romano*, 9 June 2007, licensed by author.

0.7 – Hernan Valencia, 4-5 June 1986, retrieved online (13 July 2018) at: <www. flickr.com/photos/hernanvalencias/2595523261>.

0.8 – Istvan Szucs, 16 October 2004, retrieved online (13 July 2018) at: <www. flickr.com/photos/istvanszucs/3803258215>.

0.9 – Diocese of Winona-Rochester, 2004, courtesy of emeritus Bishop Bernard Harrington via editor of *Courier*.

0.10 – Instagram, April 2017, retrieved online (April 2017) at: <www. instagram.com/p/BS19vZyBf4N/>.

0.11 – Residenza Paolo VI, retrieved online (13 July 2018) at: <d1vp8 nomjxwyf1.cloudfront.net/wp-content/uploads/sites/246/2017/10/18111731/ Terrazza-bandiera1.jpg>.

0.12 – Retrieved online (13 July 2018) at: <www.flickr.com/photos/ pejrm/42337825661>.

0.13 – Retrieved online (13 July 2018) at: <centrostuditeologici.blogspot. com/2010/12/berlusconi-ha-riottenuto-una-risicata.html>.

0.14 – CNS photo/Paul Haring, retrieved online (21 July 2018) at: <www. catholicsun.org/2015/09/23/el-papa-hijo-de-una-familia-de-inmigrantes-le-dice-a- obama-que-esta-listo-para-aprender-en-los-eeuu/>.

Figure 1.1. The emblem of the papacy: the tiara and keys

Figure 1.2. Papal States map with dates of annexation to nascent Italy

Chapter 1
Toward the Modern Papal Colors (1800–1825)

Overview

Roman Catholicism is among the world's chief religions, and its pope enjoys a unique prerogative: civil sovereignty. This is reflected by a temporal state; for the Bishop of Rome must be free from secular rulers for the sake of his ecclesial office, the "Holy See" (official parlance for the seat of the papacy and its offices—i.e., "Holy Roman Apostolic See"). Though not an article of faith, sovereignty protects the papacy from vying or intrusive world powers, and frees it for its sacred mission: to guide the universal church founded by Jesus Christ.

For centuries this spiritual mission has been signified by papal symbols—especially the keys referenced by Jesus when he promised Simon Peter, "I will give you the keys of the kingdom of heaven, and whatever you bind on earth shall be bound in heaven, and whatever you loose on earth shall be loosed in heaven" (Matthew 16:19). By the Middle Ages, these metaphorical keys appeared in the coats of arms of Peter's successors, the Bishops of Rome; and the flag with Peter's keys now flies over the sovereign papal territory where the apostle is buried: Vatican City State.

As the keys reflect the pope's spiritual mission, a tiara recalls his innate sovereignty.[1] Together they compose the papacy's longtime heraldic emblem, traditionally rendered in gold and silver (Fig. 1.1). These "tinctures" led to the modern papal colors of yellow and white, for in heraldry, gold equates with yellow and silver with white. In 1808 these colors first appeared in a papal cockade of white and yellow (see Fig. 1.27). These circular cloth badges signified political loyalties in 19th-century Europe; and within two decades, the yellow-white colors adorned Papal States flags (see Chapter 2). These all but vanished as the emerging Kingdom of Italy absorbed the Papal States between 1859 and 1870 (see map, Fig. 1.2); but when the Lateran Treaty established

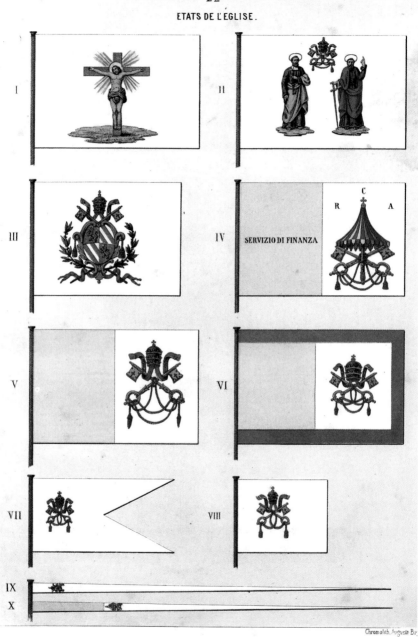

Figure 1.3. Papal States flags, 1858 (M. A. LeGras): I. Sovereign's Ensign;
II. War/Naval Ensign; III. Fort Flag; IV. State Ensign; V. Civil Ensign;
VI. Pilot Ensign; VII. Command Pennant; VIII. Naval Jack; IX. Commissioning
Streamer; X. Coast Guard Streamer

Vatican City in 1929, the new state revived a yellow-white flag flown by the papal merchant fleet in the 1800s (see Fig. 1.3, no. V).

Thus 1800 is a fitting year to begin a study of modern "papal flags"—the shorthand designation for Papal States flags and today's Vatican flag. (In fact, despite this book's title, the term "Vatican flag" was unknown before 1929.) Earlier flags have already been documented within the constraints of available sources, as has papal heraldry;[2] but the 19th century is a useful starting point for a systematic flag study for two reasons. First, it saw the rise of the modern papacy's colors and flags, in the wake of the French Revolution (1789) and its ominous implications for papal sovereignty, and second, various records are more available.

However, the research is not always easy. In the first systematic study a century ago, a French flag scholar lamented that "no work exists on pontifical flags at all, and it is also very difficult to deal with this part of the pontifical court, despite its importance".[3] Although recent authors have fared better, sometimes our knowledge remains incomplete.

Current papal flag studies, written chiefly in Italian, have limitations.[4] Some are based on the era's flag books and charts, which served as navigation resources. They thus focused on maritime flags (known as ensigns) and vary in their reliability. Other studies treat only land-based papal military colors, treating them as part of the 19th-century Italian *Risorgimento*, or "revival"—a political and military campaign to unite Italy's progenitor princely states into one.

By contrast, our present aim is a comprehensive survey of all papal flags used officially from 1800 to the present day, whether on land or at sea.[5] Primary sources are cited as much as possible, including actual flag specimens, government decrees, or eyewitness descriptions and illustrations. But there are several challenges to overcome.

First, the Papal States flew multiple flags for various functions, but not a uniform national flag.[6] This concept, now taken for granted, was still emerging there as elsewhere. Unlike today, the term "papal flag" *(bandiera pontificia)* conveyed no uniform design, but only a symbolic principle—namely, papal sovereignty—for monarchies associated flags and statehood with the sovereign. Indeed the plural term "papal flags" was also acceptable (as in Fig. 1.4).[7] While several had yellow and white vertical stripes, the term "papal flag" never implied a uniform design until Vatican City was created in 1929 and began using a state flag.

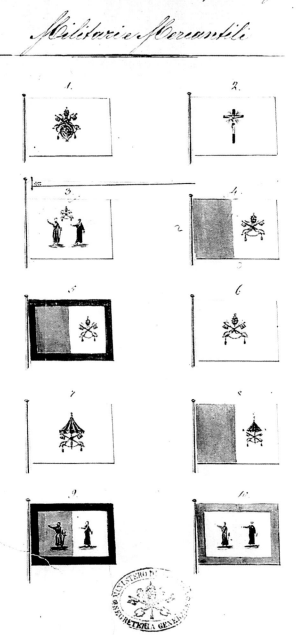

Figure 1.4. "Chart of Naval and Merchant Marine Papal Flags" (Papal States Finance Ministry, ca. 1855–1870)

Consequently there are many different Papal States flags to catalog: civil ensigns (for merchant ships), state ensigns (for customs vessels), war ensigns (for warships), civil flags (for popular use), fort flags (or "war flags"), and military colors for armed units (especially the infantry). Despite similarities, each papal flag served a distinct time period and function, and new discoveries are possible (see charts in Appendices I & II). Nor did 19th-century flag usage equate with that of today. Mass production was unknown then and some customs had yet to evolve, such as flying flags at state offices or schools. Moreover, since state rule was dispersed among differing papal agents, some flags represented papal authority without clearly bearing the title, such as those carried by special militias or the Standard of the Holy Roman Church.

A further challenge is that papal flag artifacts and documents are dispersed among numerous museums and archives in Italy and elsewhere. In some cases these can be corroborated by contemporary vexillological sources like flag books or charts, government decrees, or journalists' accounts. In other cases, available documentation provides a reasonable footing, but a less sure one. Hence a patient understanding of available sources is necessary.

For 19th-century Papal States ensigns, the principal reputable printed sources (detailed in the Works Cited) include: *Pavillons*, an 1819 French flag book, with an undated annex from a later edition; an 1825 flag decree by the pope's cardinal chamberlain;[8] *Verzameling*, a Dutch manuscript based on a dispatch from the Netherlands' ambassador in Rome in 1834;[9] a quite reliable French flag book by M. A. LeGras in 1858 (Fig. 1.3);[10] and *Quadro*, a papal flag chart furnished to foreign powers by the Papal States finance ministry between 1855 and 1870, perhaps no later than 1858 (Fig. 1.4).[11]

For land-based papal flags, valuable information on military colors and standards is furnished by the Piroli Collection *(Raccolta Piroli)*—a collection of watercolors portraying 19th-century Roman uniforms and flags. Named for its primary artist, it is preserved at the Museo Centrale del Risorgimento in Rome. Also in Rome, the Capitoline Museum and the Vatican Historical Museum at the Lateran Palace preserve several flags of the era,[12] as do public and private collections elsewhere. Appendix III provides an inventory of surviving flag specimens.

Before examining the flags attested in these varied sources, a brief retrospective on papal temporal sovereignty is needed for context.

The History of Papal Sovereignty

As the Roman Empire dissolved in the early Middle Ages, the Roman popes assumed civil rule over substantial land tracts in Europe, especially on the Italian peninsula (which became a patchwork of princely states). Known in Italian as *lo Stato Pontificio* (the Pontifical State) or *lo Stato della Chiesa* (the Church State), the country is commonly rendered in English as "the Papal States", "the States of the Church", or even "the Roman States".

With its capital at Rome, the Papal States in the 1800s comprised the Italian regions of Lazio, Umbria, The Marches, and Romagna, including the cities of Rome, Perugia, Ancona, Bologna, and Ravenna. Though small in area—roughly the size of the Netherlands (ca. 16,000 square miles)—its impact on Italian history was significant due to Italian Catholicism and the consequent role of its popes.

These included Pius VI and Pius VII, both of whom were taken prisoner during French invasions; Leo XII and Pius VIII, both of whom reigned briefly; and Gregory XVI and Pius IX, both of whom contended with the challenges of modernity and internal rebellions stemming from the *Risorgimento*.[13] (See Appendix VII for their reigns.)

The *Risorgimento* was a movement for pan-Italian unity akin to other European revolutions of the era. It ended in 1870 with the peninsula's unification under an Italian king—the last holdout being papal Rome. Its roots lay in the French Revolution (1789), after which France expanded its reach into the Italian peninsula and soon seized the Papal States, declared a Roman Republic (1796), and exiled Pius VI to France, where he died in 1799.

That year, compelled to withdraw, France surrendered the Papal States, minus some territory. The Kingdom of the Two Sicilies (i.e., Naples) administered Rome until 1800 when it was turned over to a new pope, Pius VII. He was deported in 1808 when France again occupied the Papal States, at the instigation of Napoleon (who likewise aided the previous invasion). After Napoleon's defeat in 1814, the Congress of Vienna revived the Papal States; but because he had successfully united the peninsula for a time, pan-Italian nationalism was born—stoking local uprisings which eventually climaxed in Italy's unification. The cause was led by the House of Savoy in the Kingdom of Sardinia, which ruled that island and the region around Turin known as Piedmont.

Political uprisings in the Papal States erupted in 1831, 1848–1849, and 1859–1860. In the last one Piedmont seized two-thirds of papal lands when the pope's Austrian protectors withdrew. His northern cities (Bologna, Ravenna) fell in 1859, while outlying cities (Ancona, Perugia) fell in 1860 after a decisive loss at Castelfidardo. Thereafter his territory was reduced to Rome and the surrounding region of Lazio, defended by French troops. Soon that too would be lost.

In 1861 the Kingdom of Italy was formed by Victor Emmanuel II of the House of Savoy, uniting the entire peninsula except San Marino (which remains independent today), Venice (which joined Italy in 1866), and papal Rome. He established his capital at Florence in 1865, and pledged not to attack Rome, but this fueled a rivalry between Italian royalists and republicans. The latter included firebrands like Giuseppe Garibaldi, whose militia tried to seize Rome in 1867. Franco-Papal forces defeated him at Mentana. But when France withdrew its Roman garrison to fight Prussia, Italian forces seized the city on 20 September 1870, and declared it the nation's capital.

Statistics clearly show the decline of the Papal States in the 1800s.[14] Its population approached 3 million before territorial losses in 1859–1860 reduced it to 1 million. Its 17th-century army of 50,000 diminished sharply by the time of the French Revolution. During civil unrest in 1843, it stood at 20,000, and by 1870 it had declined again by half. In the 1800s it also relied on foreign volunteers, as well as native garrisons from France and Austria. Papal Rome, the capital and "city of the apostles", held 160,000 souls at mid-century; and its loss in 1870 proved irreversible.

The seizure of papal Rome resulted in the sixty-year "Roman Question" period, during which successive popes styled themselves "prisoners of the Vatican" and remained cloistered behind its walls. They rejected the Italian "Law of Guarantees" which gave them practical jurisdiction over Vatican palaces— but not full sovereignty.

The matter was resolved in 1929 by the Lateran Accords *(Patti Lateranensi)* between Italy and the Holy See. These comprised a concordat regularizing the church's role in Italy and the Lateran Treaty. In the treaty, the pope abandoned his claims to the former Papal States and recognized the Kingdom of Italy. The Holy See in turn acquired a financial indemnity, sovereignty over the new "Vatican City State", and extraterritorial immunity for papal offices and shrines elsewhere in Rome. The logic presumes the Holy See to

Figure 1.5. Standard of the Church, 1571 (Ship Replica, Admiral of the Fleet, detail)

be a sovereign international power entitled to the legal attributes of such status, currently understood as statehood. Tiny by design, the Vatican state thus enshrines and guarantees the Holy See's sovereign rights.

Thus fared the sovereignty of the popes, whose flag designs formed two categories in the 1800s. At first white flags bearing papal emblems were flown— flags inherited from previous centuries. These are examined in Chapter 1, concluding with a new yellow-and-white papal cockade (1808). The latter in turn inspired yellow-and-white flags, first at sea primarily, and then on land. These are examined in Chapter 2. Chapter 3 treats flags of the Roman Question period (1870–1929), the Vatican flag itself (since 1929), and the laws and customs surrounding papal flags today. Finally, several Appendices provide summary flag charts by pontificate; a roster of actual Papal States flag specimens and dimensions; official decrees; and other details.

White Flags and Ensigns

Well before the 19th century, Papal States flags were characterized by white fields. These had long replaced older, red papal banners known since the Middle Ages. The latter deserve a brief word since they were the progenitors of papal flags reviewed in the present study.

Recorded papal flags were first typified by the "Standard of the Holy Roman Church" (whose 19th-century form will be examined later). Conveying church authority, these banners came to be identified with the pope as the church's head, and became de facto papal flags.[15] From the Middle Ages, they flew from papal installations, or were consigned to Christian princes or military commanders as a sacred augury and a sign of papal favor. They had various designs, were often red (until the 1600s or so) with tails or other appendages, and bore various religious charges.[16]

One version featured representations of Jesus crucified and/or the apostles buried in Rome, Ss. Peter and Paul. A famous example is held in Gaeta, whose cathedral claims to preserve the standard presented by Pius V to Marcantonio Colonna in 1571 for the naval Battle of Lepanto. It is an ornate reddish vexillum bearing the crucifixion scene, with the apostles on either side, shown here in a replica ship (Fig. 1.5).[17] A second version featured the pontiff's personal arms and/or the Petrine keys. Early on the keys perhaps appeared alone,[18] but

Figure 1.6. Papal Banner at Castel Sant'Angelo, Rome (watercolor/engraving, detail, ca. 1790 [anachronistic])

Figure 1.7. Papal Flag Patterns: medieval to modern

were later surmounted by the ceremonial umbrella that was carried before the pope, or by his tiara. These flags are attested in contemporary prints of Rome's major fortress, Castel Sant'Angelo (as in Fig. 1.6, which is anachronistic).[19]

By 1700 or so, these red flags came to have white fields (and after 1825, yellow-and-white fields; see Fig. 1.7[20])—but the charges upon them remained basically the same, as evidenced by flags illustrated here. The catalyst for white fields was France's "royal standard", which was white with various royal charges (or none at all). It originated in the mid-1600s and flew from warships and forts in France and its colonies, influencing the flags of several European monarchies in turn.[21] After the French Revolution and its promotion throughout Europe under the new *Tricolore*, white flags further symbolized royalty's resistance to revolution or secular republicanism, including in the Papal States.[22]

Indeed, by the end of the Congress of Vienna in 1815 papal rule and its attendant white flags had twice been restored to Rome after two French occupations involving Napoleon. These flags appear in maritime flag sources such as *Pavillons* (1819), the *Verzameling* dispatches (1834), LeGras' book (1858), and the Papal States government chart, *Quadro*. Comparisons show slight changes in exact designs or usage. Before 1800 flag sources are unclear on precise flag usage; but *Pavillons* (1819) clearly distinguishes merchant from naval ensigns. Modern studies suggest either the election of Pius VII (1803) or his return to Rome from exile (1815) occasioned papal flag revival or standardized use, but an explicit papal act has yet to be cited.[23]

Among these white flags, one was the "Reigning Pope's Flag" and bore in the center his personal arms (i.e., family arms), augmented by the papal tiara and keys and (often) a wreath.[24] The arms were moved toward the hoist to increase visibility. It thus resembled the flags of other European sovereigns whose standards were white with the respective royal arms. It flew at Papal States forts and garrison sites, including major city squares, and was thus a fort flag (Italian, *bandiera da fortezza*). Indirectly it also represented civil agents nearby, since state flags for such offices do not seem attested in the Papal States.[25] At sea this flag could also be used by merchant ships, until a new design replaced it in 1825. Its maritime use is well-attested from at least the early 17th century.[26]

The 1819 *Pavillons* labelled this flag as one of two alternate civil ensigns, bearing the arms of Pius VII (Fig. 1.8).[27] An 1822 print shows the same flag flying from the Milvian Bridge watchtowers near Rome (Fig. 1.9).[28] Use at such forts is recorded in 1834 by the *Verzameling*, where it bears the arms of Gregory

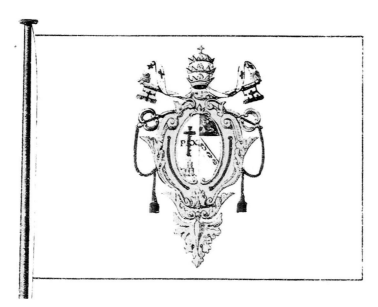

Figure 1.8. Fort flag & alternate Civil Ensign, 1819, Pius VII

Figure 1.9. Fort flag, Milvian Bridge, ca. 1822 (lithograph detail)

Figure 1.10. Fort flag, 1834, Gregory XVI

Figure 1.11. Ceremonial flag, Gregory XVI

Figure 1.12. Fort flag, 1858, Pius IX

Figure 1.13. Militia color, 1847, Pius IX

XVI (Fig. 1.10).[29] An actual flag of this design is held by the Museum of the Risorgimento in Milan (Fig. 1.11).[30] Gregory's arms are painted upon a plain white field and adorned with an angelic face beneath the tiara. Nearly square and made of silk, it bears yellow and white fringe on three sides. While these elements often typify military colors, its design is different from and larger than those attested in Rome (to be examined later). It may have been a ceremonial fort flag or garrison flag.

An 1835 watercolor shows this flag flying from the foremast of the warship schooner, *San Pietro*, and another nearby (see Fig. 1.21).[31] LeGras confirmed this (1858) and stated that it was "hoisted on all forts of the States of the Church, and at the mizzenmast of all warships, on high feast days only". He named it the "Reigning Pontiff's Ensign"; here it bears the arms of Pius IX (Fig. 1.12).[32] A small ceremonial flag of this design is preserved by the Museo del Risorgimento in Ravenna (Fig. 1.13).[33] Dating from 1847, it is made of silk with a painted emblem, and has yellow and white fringe. Though its precise usage is unclear, it bears a Roman numeral likely alluding to an armed unit, and resembles contemporary flags assigned to civic militias in Rome and Bologna. These will be described later, along with yellow-white fort flags used before papal Rome fell.[34]

A second white flag, bearing the tiara and keys alone, is recorded as an alternate civil ensign in the 1819 *Pavillons*. Such use was known from at least the 18th century. Later sources also attest it as a harbor service flag and a naval jack (Fig. 1.14).[35] One jack specimen is held by the Vatican Historical Museum (Fig. 1.15),[36] and belonged to the corvette *Immacolata Concezione*. She was retained at Civitavecchia for several years after papal Rome's fall in 1870, should the pope opt for exile.[37] The tiara-and-keys emblem is painted slightly hoistward of the flag's center, doubtless to enhance visibility. Both keys are golden-yellow. At times, this design is also reported at forts, instead of the appointed white flag with the reigning pontiff's personal arms.[38]

A third white flag served as a war ensign. A simple form dates at the latest to the late 1600s: a white flag bearing images of the apostles Peter (holding a key) and Paul (holding a sword); perhaps merchant ships used it too.[39] After 1800 sources show it as a naval ensign only and add a tiara-and-keys emblem at top-center. The 1819 *Pavillons* showed golden adornments in the corners, but these might be artistic license and atypical (Fig. 1.16).[40] LeGras showed it without adornments (1858), and with more prominent effigies, each upon his

Figure 1.14. Naval Jack, 1858

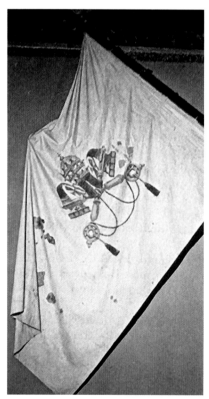

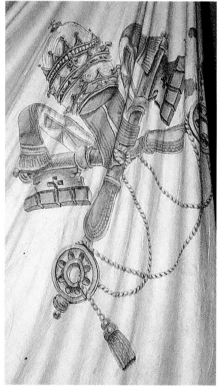

Figure 1.15a. Naval Jack,
Immacolata Concezione, *1870*

Figure 1.15b. Naval Jack, 1870, detail

Figure 1.16. War Ensign, 1819

Figure 1.17. War Ensign, 1858

Figure 1.18. War Ensign, 1860, San Pietro

Figure 1.19a. War Ensign, 1870,
Immacolata Concezione

Figure 1.19b. War Ensign, 1870,
Immacolata Concezione

Figure 1.20. War Ensign (above stern), 1860, Immacolata Concezione

own mound, (Fig. 1.17).[41] LeGras also describes two naval pennants: a command-pennant and a commissioning-streamer (see Fig. 1.3, nos. VII & IX).

Two war ensign specimens are held by the Vatican Historical Museum at the Lateran Palace in Rome. One belonged to the papal military steamer *San Pietro* which surrendered with honors to Italian forces at Ancona on 26 September 1860 (Fig. 1.18), and the other to the aforementioned *Immacolata Concezione* (Fig. 1.19).[42] On the latter both Petrine keys are golden-yellow but on the former, one is silver; and the figures are all painted. Contemporary art also attests the war ensign. It flies above the stern of the *Immacolata Concezione* in a rare 1860 photo (Fig. 1.20),[43] while an older watercolor shows it worn by an earlier ship, also named *San Pietro* (Fig. 1.21).[44]

A fourth white flag served as the sovereign's ensign when a pope was aboard ship. The 1819 *Pavillons* calls it the "Ensign of the Holy Church", and shows it as a white flag bearing a crucifix flanked by the apostles Peter (flyward with the keys) and Paul (hoistward with the sword), along with floral ornamentations (Fig. 1.22).[45] In 1858 the LeGras illustration featured only the crucifix centered on a white field (Fig. 1.23).[46] (The *Verzameling* recorded a similar flag with a red field for display "in battle"; but the government chart *Quadro* does not confirm this, and the concept likely dates from an earlier era.[47])

Figure 1.21. War Ensign & Pontiff's Ensign, 1835, Papal schooner San Pietro, *Civitavecchia (M. Fonda, watercolor)*

Figure 1.22. Sovereign's Ensign, 1819

Figure 1.23. Sovereign's Ensign, 1858

LeGras called this flag a "Papal Ensign" (*Pavillon Papal*) hoisted "at the mainmast of warships when His Holiness the Pope is aboard", as well as "on the rowboat that carries His Holiness" or "at a twenty-one-gun salute".[48] It thus signified the presence of the church's temporal head, the "Vicar of Christ", as illustrated by the crucifix. At least once it also flew at his coastal residence: in 1862 an eyewitness reported it flying above a seaside palace loggia in Anzio, where Pius IX prayed amid his troops, within sight of a warship (which presumably loaned its ensign for display ashore).[49] By contrast, at inland residences, artists and historians attest only the Swiss Guard's striped flag (examined later), both at the Quirinal Palace and near the Vatican's Bronze Doors (Figs. 1.24–25).[50]

During a vacant see after a pope died, 19th-century sources report that warships flew a white flag with an umbrella surmounting the keys, probably at the foremast (Fig. 1.26, with a corresponding streamer at the main).[51] This emblem recalls the ceremonial umbrella once carried before popes in procession and often found today in pontifical basilicas, as an insignia of the Roman church and its temporal power. Since the latter was supervised by the cardinal chamberlain (*camerlengo*), he has long employed the umbrella-and-keys emblem as his insignia—especially on coins and seals during a vacant see (still true today). His insignia might also appear combined with the pontiff's personal arms to represent state authority when the see was full.

The umbrella emblem (*ombrellino*) is also known by other names, such as gonfalon (*gonfalone*), pavilion (*padiglione*), and baldachin (*baldacchino*). For many centuries its hood has been rendered in an alternating pattern of red and yellow (or gold).[52] As seen previously, these colors featured in past papal and ecclesiastical standards; and from 1800 to 1808 they were the colors of papal Rome's cockade, as well.

The Papal Cockade

Political loyalties in 19th-century Europe were often signified by a cockade, a cloth badge composed of several colors, often in concentric circles. The "Roman Republic", sponsored by French forces who exiled Pius VI, first introduced a black, white, and red cockade on 16 February 1798. After papal rule was restored, Pius VII replaced it in July 1800 with the first-ever papal cockade, of red and yellow,[53] time-honored Roman and ecclesiastical colors. The

Figure 1.24. Swiss Guard Flag, Quirinal Palace, artwork undated

Figure 1.25. Swiss Guard Flag, Piazza S. Pietro, photo ca. 1860

cockade lasted only eight years, but the colors are still preserved in the modern flag of the Commune of Rome—a vertical bicolor of maroon (amaranth-red) and golden-yellow.[54]

In 1808 France reoccupied the Papal States. In protest Pius VII again adopted a new cockade, this time of yellow and white. The sole surviving specimen is preserved by Spain's embassy to the Holy See, as pictured in a 1908 Vatican booklet (Fig. 1.27; the seam is splitting).[55] This yellow-white papal cockade is considered the origin of the modern papal colors, and proved to be of long-lasting significance, since its colors eventually inspired the designs of many papal flags, including today's Vatican flag.

The French reoccupation began in January 1808 under the guise of temporary passage. However, by February French cannon were aimed at the papal palace on the Quirinal Hill and by March the exile or imprisonment of papal functionaries was commonplace and papal troops were being absorbed into the French army.[56]

A contemporary diary reports that in protest, the pope issued the yellow-white cockade on 13 March 1808 to the militias still loyal to him: the Noble Guard, the Swiss Guard, the Campidoglio Militia, and the Guardia di Finanza.[57] In this way, papal loyalists would no longer be wearing the same red-yellow colors as the Roman troops who had acquiesced to the occupation. Three days later the papal secretary of state also asked diplomats in Rome accredited to the Holy See to wear the new cockade:

> To Foreign Ministers, from the Halls of the Quirinal,
> 16 March 1808.
>
> ... After such violent incorporation, and the said Troop continuing to carry the same Pontifical Cockade, His Holiness, not having in the current circumstances other means to render public his dissent, and ... deciding not to have any part in the operations of the said incorporated Troop, which he no longer recognizes as his own, has made the decision of changing the Cockade and of having it distributed to the small number of the troop remaining to him in Rome.
>
> His Holiness, wishing this to be known by Y[our] E[xcellency] in order [that Your Excellency may] be carried

Figure 1.26. Vacant See Ensign, 1834

Figure 1.27. Papal Cockade, 1808

Figure 1.28. Papal Cockade of yellow and white, Civic Guard hat, undated

Figure 1.29. Papal Cockade of gold and silver, Legione Bolognese hat, 1848/1849

unto recognition at his Court, has ordered Cardinal Doria
Pamphili, Pro-Secretary of State, to make your own this formal
participation, and to enclose a sample of said new cockade ….[58]

France retaliated by assigning the new cockade to its sympathizers in
the former papal army. Pius protested this to the French command and his
diplomatic corps. Upon learning of Napoleon's displeasure at the new papal
cockade, the French command falsely claimed that Pius himself gave it to his
diplomatic community and former army—when in fact the latter received it
from the French.[59]

Soon cockades in the Italian and French colors were worn to promote a
unified Italy under Napoleon. Protesting orders to abandon the papal cockade,
a papal officer in Ancona averred that he would rather die than fail to honor
"this flag which waved gloriously yesterday for my return to this city".[60] (The
flag's design is uncertain.[61])

The meaning of the new cockade's yellow-white colors is not documented,[62]
but they were likely derived from a longstanding traditional papal emblem, the
gold and silver keys of Peter.[63] By heraldic custom and for display on cloth, gold
and silver are replaced by yellow and white. This logic is reiterated by the previous Roman colors, red and yellow, which may have stemmed from medieval
renditions of the papal keys in gold on a red shield. These colors thus figured
in the traditional emblem of the Roman Senate and People (SPQR) as well as
the ceremonial pontifical umbrella.

Both keys were often gold or yellow in 19th-century arms and flags, but the
tiara's core was always silver or white, thus retaining dual colors for the compos-
ite emblem. It is uncertain when dual-colored keys became the heraldic norm,
but literature and art attest the concept early on. Around 1300 Dante described
the keys as gold and silver, or as yellow and white;[64] and around 1481 Perugino
painted Christ bequeathing a key in each color to St. Peter.[65] By Vatican City's
creation in 1929, dual-colored keys had become fixed in papal arms and flags.

The yellow-white papal cockade was abolished when Napoleon annexed
the Papal States. The decree, signed secretly on 17 May 1809, was announced
in Rome on 10 June. That morning at Castel Sant'Angelo fortress, the French
tricolor replaced the papal flag (or arms—sources vary).[66] In response, Pius VII
excommunicated Napoleon, who in turn arrested the pope in July, and exiled him.

Figure 1.30. Bicolor flag atop Castel Sant'Angelo (ca. 1815), painted by C. W. Eckersberg (original, ca. 1815)

Figure 1.31. Bicolor flag atop Castel Sant'Angelo (ca. 1815) (detail of artist's later reproduction, 1818)

After Napoleon abdicated in 1814, the Papal States were restored in May by a papal legate, in Lazio and Umbria only. Pius VII returned to Rome on 24 May, and the Congress of Vienna reconstituted his remaining Italian lands in June 1815. In consequence the yellow-white cockade was fully restored,[67] but over time was rendered differently. Instead of appearing side-by-side, the colors were usually displayed concentrically—yellow (or gold) on the inside and white (or silver) on the outside (Figs. 1.28–29).[68]

The previous suite of papal flags was likewise restored. Indeed, on 11 May 1814, as the papal legate's mandate began, the papal flag was ceremoniously hoisted at Castel Sant'Angelo fortress.[69] But its design is uncertain; around 1815, a painting records a new flag atop the fort, a bicolor that may be yellow over white (Fig. 1.30).[70] In the painting by C. W. Eckersberg, held by the National Gallery of Denmark, the yellow stripe appears reddish-orange. Shortly afterward, he reproduced his work, again featuring the fort's flag (Fig. 1.31, held privately)[71] along with vertical white banners at the bastions. The latter often appear in artwork of the era: a white vexillum bearing the pontiff's personal arms at one Tiber River bastion, opposite another bearing the umbrella-and-keys emblem of the *camerlengo*.[72]

If represented accurately, Eckersberg's work may provide the earliest example of a yellow-and-white papal flag—which may be an anomaly, because further confirmation of such "bicolor" fort flags is lacking until mid-century.[73] In any case, within a decade the Papal States explicitly adopted flags in these colors for use at sea. Their emergence is documented in the next chapter, along with the subsequent migration of bicolor flags ashore.

Notes, Chapter 1

1. This is true even in the flags or arms of several republics: Russia, Hungary, Serbia, San Marino, etc.

2. Ziggioto, "Le bandiere degli stati italiani," part I. Erdmann. Bascapè "Drapeaux pontificaux". Galbreath.

3. "Drapeaux pontificaux", p. 95.

4. Cf. Vigevano, Ziggioto, Colangeli, Ales, Fiora, Brandani, et al.

5. Cf. Becker: "The Adoption of the Flag of the Vatican City State, 1929", "The Flag of Vatican City", "Papal States Flags, 1800–1870", "The Proto-National Papal Flag", "The Vatican Flag: Proportions & Alternatives", and "Vatican Flags".

6. Neighboring Italian states tended to have more uniform designs despite their varying functions; cf. LeGras.

7. *Quadro* bears ten different Papal States ensigns designated overall as "Naval and Merchant Marine Papal Flags" (*Bandiere pontificie di marina militari e mercantili*). Note the plural—as also in the 1825 decree by Pierfrancesco Galleffi adopting new maritime ensigns to establish "uniformity in the colors and forms of the Papal Flags [sic] which are ... hoisted by [Papal] State[s] Ships" (see pp. 37–38 and Appendix IV).

8. See pp. 37–38 and Appendix IV.

9. *Verzameling* features several Papal States flags in a folio titled "Italie. Romeinische Staat." documented by the Netherlands ambassador to Rome in his dispatch of 29 April 1834. These include: (10) the fort flag (also for naval use on feast days at the foremast); (11) the war ensign; (12) a battle ensign and streamer (with a red field); (13) the Vacant See flag and pennant; (14) the state ensign and streamer; (15) the harbor service flag (later, the jack) and pennant; (16) the civil ensign; (17) the pilot ensign; and (18) a plain yellow-white vertical bicolor identified as "the Roman signal flag for communication with the shore".

10. LeGras, pl. 22.

11. *Quadro delle Bandiere Pontificie di Marina Militari e Mercantili*, bears the stamp of the Secretary General of the Papal States Finance Ministry; black & white photo of an undated chart (between 1855 & 1870) from the pontificate of Pius IX, in the Whitney Smith Flag Research Center Collection archives, University of Texas at Austin, acquired from the archives of Dr. Ottfried Neubecker (acquired in turn from the German admiralty). Though undated, it bears several clues: the coat of arms (no. 1) reflects the pontificate of Pius IX (1846–1878); the award flags were adopted in 1855 (nos. 9–10); and since LeGras closely parallels its contents in 1858, it may have been issued before then; perhaps when naval and customs fleets merged (1856). Although identifying text is lost, it clearly shows: (1) fort flag, which also flew from the foremast of warships on feast days; (2) Sovereign's ensign (with a white field); (3) war ensign surmounted by commissioning pennant; (4) civil ensign; (5) pilot ensign; (6) jack; (7) Vacant See ensign; (8) state ensign; (9) first-class award flag for merchant ship captains; and (10) second-class award flag for merchant ship captains.

12. Located at the Vatican until 1987, the Museo Storico Vaticano is now located at the Lateran Palace in Rome, which is attached to the basilica of the same name. It opened in its new location in 1991.

13. Galbreath, pp. 103–105, details the coats of arms of these popes.

14. Cf. Vigevano 1–45; Andrieux, p. 36f; Donovan, pp. 1012–1015; Ziggioto, "Le bandiere degli stati italiani," part I, p. 123; Bouquet; Alvarez. Moreover, in 1793 the papal navy had

about twenty armed vessels; but by 1870 had diminished by half, including customs vessels. In 1829 the papal merchant marine had 91 vessels for foreign trade, and many coasters and fishing craft; but by 1870, only 271 small boats.

15. The growing association of the Standard with papal authority is shown in 1669 in connection with the Battle of Candia against the Turks: the pope granted a red standard that bore his personal arms between figures of the apostles Peter and Paul. When a courtier observed that the pontiff's personal arms removed the standard's status as "of the church," the papal envoy replied that "his master could not separate himself from the church, and that for this reason it was appropriate that his arms be in the center between the apostles" ("Drapeaux pontificaux", p. 98).

16. "Drapeaux pontificaux," pp. 95–98. Holy See Press Office. Galbreath, pp. 58–62. Erdmann. Ziggioto, "Le bandiere degli stati italiani," part I, pp. 108–112. *Flags of the World 1669–1670*, plates 1 and 3. Van Dijk.

17. Illustration from "La Galea Ammiraglia della Flotta Pontificia nella Battaglia di Lepanto (1571),"Associazione Culturale "Gaeta e il Mare," retrieved online (1 August 2010) at <www. gaetaeilmare.it/modelli/Galea/Galea.htm> and available via <archive.org>. Cf. also, "La battaglia di Lepanto, Gaeta e la Confraternità del SS. Rosario", retrieved online (1 August 2010) at: <www.golfotv.info/home/content/view/984/29/> and available via <archive.org>.

18. Cf. Becker, "Papal States Flags, 1803–1870", cover and p. 204 (with reference to the Villani Manuscript, Chigi Codex, Biblioteca Apostolica Vaticana: viz. a 15th or 16th century record of a battle near Giglio Island in 1241). Cf. also, Galbreath, pp. 6–16.

19. "Le Pont Saint Ange à Rome; Pont et Chateau St. Ange à Rome", watercolor/engraving, Chez Hocquart, Paris, ca. 1790 (anachronistic), retrieved online (12 June 2018) at: <www. edition-originale.com/en/travel/europa/-vue-doptique-pont-et-chateau-saint-1790-45607>. The main flagpole is typically adorned with a red swallow-tailed flag bearing the Petrine keys, usually surmounted by a gonfalon or tiara. Upon the river bastions can be seen two further banners, one typically bearing the pontiff's personal arms, and the other bearing the umbrella-keys. Cf. "Drapeaux pontificaux", p. 98.

20. Thumbnail illustrations used or adapted from Roberto Breschi, retrieved online (25 June 2018) at: <www.rbvex.it/chiesa.html>.

21. Smith, *Flags Through the Ages and Across the World*, pp. 133–134.

22. For another interpretation of the white color, cf. Lovell: "as stated by St. Clement of Alexandria, white is 'tintura veritatis', (color of truth) and the Pope is the only master of truth in the world."

23. Secondary sources state that papal flag-restoration orders were issued in 1803 and 1815, but the author was unable to confirm this in the collection of Papal States decrees at the Biblioteca Casanatense in Rome. Pagliucchi, 'Bandiere Pontificie,' specifies a Notification of the *Camerlengo*, 22 December 1803, establishing the war ensign and sovereign's ensign as in *Pavillons*; along with two civil ensigns—one bearing the tiara-and-keys for "navi di commercio", and one bearing the umbrella-keys for "bastimenti mercantili" (the latter replaced in *Pavillons* by one with the pontiff's personal arms). Cf. Ziggioto, "Le bandiere degli stati italiani", part I, 113 & 115 (specifies 1803 and again on 7 June 1815—the second return of Pius VII to Rome after a brief refuge in Genoa, his first return having been in May 1814); Ferrari, p. 84; Rangoni-Machiavelli, p. 76; Breschi; Denis-Delacour, p. 402–403.

24. The wreath was perhaps influenced by other sovereign coats of arms of the era, although similar floral decorations around the shield were used at least as early as the reign of Sixtus IV (1471–1484), albeit without any indication that they appeared on a contemporary flag.

25. See p. 59.

26. Ziggioto, "Le bandiere degli stati italiani", part I, p. 111, lists the flag manuscript by J. Moutton (ca. 1670) as the earliest witness, but notes that the flag portrayed (for "papal galleys") is older still, carrying the arms of Urban VIII (1623–44). A 1741 Spanish manuscript (cf. *Banderas o Pabellones*, *"Papa"*) shows it bearing the arms of Benedict XIV (1740–58). A 1765 Tuscan manuscript (*Blasone marittimo*, pl. 9, "Papal Ensign [*Paviglione Pontificio*] with the arms of the Reigning Pope") shows it with the arms of Clement XIII (1758–69).

27. Illustration from *Pavillons*, pl. 8, no. 4, identified as "another merchant flag" alongside the "ordinary merchant flag" described below.

28. Illustration from author photo of lithograph held by the Pontifical North American College in Rome: Luigi Rossini, "Veduta del Ponte Molle sul Tevere", 1822, inscribed in Italian: "Rosini dis. e inc. View of Ponte Molle [Milvian Bridge] on the Tiber. Two nautical miles away from Rome. This bridge was restored, and the triumphal arch constructed, by the Supreme Pontiff Pius VII, [gloriously] reigning. Rome, 1822". Macadam, p. 257, says of the bridge: "Remodeled in the fifteenth century by Nicholas V, who added the watch towers, it was restored in 1805 by Pius VII, who commissioned Valdier to erect the triumphal arch at the entrance." Other contemporary prints of the scene likewise show the flag.

29. Illustration from *Verzameling*, no. 10, titled "Flag of the reigning pope which is hoisted on forts" ("Vlag van de regerende Paus zooals die op de Forten geheschen wordt").

30. Illustration from Centro Italiano Studi Vessillologici, "Visita al Museo del Risorgimento Milano, 7 novembre 2009", retrieved online (1 August 2010) at <www.cisv.it/viola/milano2b.html>. Colangeli, fig. 16 (who incorrectly gives the inventory number as 1150—but there is none). Emails to author from the Museo di Milano: Maura Bertoli (9, 16, & 27 April 2009) and Francesco Mereu (9 April 2009).

31. Illustration from calendar art in author's archives, M. Fonda, "La goletta San Pietro alla vela mentre esce dal porto di Civitavecchia", tempera on paper, 1835, Museo di Roma; also online (18 June 2018) at "La Marina dello Stato Pontificio", *Marina Militare—Ministero della Difesa* [Italiana] at: <www.marina.difesa.it/storiacultura/storia/storianavale/Pagine/pontificia.aspx>.

32. Illustration from LeGras, pl. 22, no. 3, "Pavillon du Pontife régnant".

33. Illustration from catalog no. 237; cf. "stendardo" entry retrieved online (18 June 2018) via <bbcc.ibc.regione.emilia-romagna.it/pater/loadcard.do?id_card=55016>.

34. See pp. 51–56, 63–64.

35. Illustration from Le Gras, pl. 22, No. 8: "Proportions 1:1.17 ... One hoists it on the bowsprit of ships of the [Papal] State[s], on feast days only. It can also serve as the command flag." In 1819 it was called the "ordinary merchant flag" and is pictured along with an alternate design, the fort flag (*Pavillons*, pl. 8, nos. 3–4). As a harbor service flag, cf. *Verzameling*, no. 15. As a civil ensign, this flag dates from at least the 18th century (e.g., Smith, *Flags Through the Ages*, p. 204, the fifth row of the chart—"Pav[illon] de Rome").

36. Illustration (crop) from author's photo, 1984; and (full) from "La Marina dello Stato Pontificio", *Marina Militare—Ministero della Difesa* [Italiana], retrieved online (18 June 2018) at: <www.marina.difesa.it/storiacultura/storia/storianavale/Pagine/pontificia.aspx>. The same photo appears in Savio, p. 58, who states that the flag was held by the Museo delle Guardie Nobili (in 1970). Brandani et al, pp. 90–91. The jack is no longer on display at the Museo Vaticano Storico (author's observations, 2009) and is unlisted in its

flag inventory (provided to author). See also below, Chapter 3 ("The Roman Question"): the flag may be that discovered in 1920, as reported by *Roma nelle fotografie della Raccolta Ceccarius*, p. 92.

37. Bouquet, pp. 75–76. Alvarez, p. 258. In 1872 the ship was transferred to the French port of Toulon, still under the papal flag, until its sale in 1878.

38. As at Civitavecchia's fort in a 19th century watercolor by Michele Fonda at the Museo di Roma, "Naval procession of Pope Gregory XVI from Civitavecchia to Saline Corneto [today Tarquinia]", May 23, 1835, De Agostini Picture Library via Getty Images, retrieved online (18 June 2018) at <www.gettyimages.com/detail/illustration/naval-procession-of-pope-gregory-xvi-from-civitavecchia-stock-graphic/163236800>. Cf. also Capefigue, p. 367 (Rome, early 1800s), Buckingham, p. 243 (Civitavecchia, 1846).

39. Ziggioto, "Le bandiere degli stati italiani", part I, p. 111 and p. 122, note 18, lists sources beginning with 1695. Several 19th century sources also document this flag, probably anachronistically. Cf. Ales, p. 394–95.

40. Illustration from *Pavillons*, pl. 8, no. 2. Rangoni-Machiavelli, p. 76. Whitney Smith has noted that the effigies closely resemble those of Plato and Aristotle in Raphael's fresco, "The School of Athens", in the Vatican Museums (letter to author, 10 November 1993).

41. Illustration from Le Gras, pl. 22, no. 2. The proportions are given as 3:4 and the citation reads: "This is the ensign of warships. Merchant ships cannot carry it anymore. It is flown from the stern of all ships belonging to the [papal] state, every day, after the rising of the sun and never after its setting."

42. Illustrations from author's photos, 1984. Cf. *Guide to the Vatican Museums*, p. 155.

43. Illustration from Collezione Achille Rastelli, image no. 1302 C retrieved online (1 August 2010) via <www.agenziabozzo.it/Ita/Navi_da_Guerra.shtm> and (18 June 2018) online at <www.agenziabozzo.it/navi_da_guerra/c-navi%20da%20guerra/C-1302_IMMACOLATA_CONCEZIONE_1860_corvetta_Marina_Pontificia_Yacht_Papale.htm>. Cf. *Roma nelle fotografie della Raccolta Ceccarius*, p. 92.

44. Illustration from calendar art, author's archives, M. Fonda, "La goletta San Pietro alla vela mentre esce dal porto di Civitavecchia", tempera on paper, 1835, Museo di Roma; also online (18 June 2018) at "La Marina dello Stato Pontificio", *Marina Militare—Ministero della Difesa* [Italiana] at: <www.marina.difesa.it/storiacultura/storia/storianavale/Pagine/pontificia.aspx>.

45. Illustration from *Pavillons*, pl. 8, no. 1 ("Flag of the Holy Church").

46. Illustration from Le Gras, pl. 22, no. 1.

47. *Verzameling*, no. 12, shows the flag with a red field set below a red streamer for use "in battle"; but *Quadro* shows it with a white field only.

48. Le Gras, no. 1 (proportions 10:17).

49. Le Chauff de Kerguenec, p. 277f, describes the Anzio scene first-hand: "a white flag which bore the image of a Crucifix". "Drapeaux pontificaux", p. 99, n. 1, reports the memory as enduring. Ziggioto, "Le bandiere degli stati italiani", part I, pp. 113–115, describes it as the "flag of the Holy Church," or the "maritime flag of the Church," noting that it came to be "raised also on land, on buildings where the pontiff was found, but—so it seems—far from Rome and generally on the coast" (p. 123, note 25). Rangoni-Machiavelli, p. 76 ("flag of the Holy See").

50. Illustration of the Quirinal Palace bastion from "Guardia Svizzera Pontificia" at facebook.com, 6 July 2014, with no information on the artist, date, or collection; retrieved online

(18 June 2018) at <www.facebook.com/gsp1506/photos/a.435356976577514.107374182 9.223853514394529/593627424083801/?type=1&relevant_count=1>. Various artwork of the period illustrates the flag at the palace similarly. Illustration of Piazza San Pietro (ca. 1860) from Gabinetto Fotografico Nazionale, Rome, retrieved online (18 June 2018) at <www.flickr.com/photos/dealvariis/5529560360>. Krieg, p. 448, reports that the flag flew outside a window near the Bronze Doors and extended into St. Peter's Square, from the era of Gregory XVI (though artwork attests it much earlier); but inside the window near the Doors, after 1870; For Guard flags, see pp. 114–115.

51. Illustration from *Verzameling*, no. 15, which states its use by naval vessels. Also pictured by *Pavillons*, pl. 9; *Flaggen Almanack*, pl. 15; and *Quadro*, no. 7. Cf. Rangoni-Machiavelli, p. 77. Occasional illustrations of a bicolor bisected by the emblem seem spurious (e.g., Ferrari, p. 84).

52. Galbreath, pp. 27–37. Heim, pp. 55–59.

53. Vigevano, pp. 69–70, and Ferrari, p. 83, note that the republic's cockade corresponded to its flag: a vertical tricolor of black-white-red. MacSwiney de Mashanaglass, p. 8.

54. Gasbarri, p. 198, sees amaranth-red as symbolic of the ecclesiastical legacy, and gold as symbolic of the Roman Empire.

55. Illustration from MacSwiney de Mashanaglass, a single colored plate titled "Fac-simile del campione della coccarda pontificia conservato nell'Archivio dell'Ambasciata di Spagna presso la Santa Sede"; cf. also ibid. pp. 11–12, n. 2. The cockade's facsimile image is approximately 10 cm (4 in.) in diameter; stitches have come unfastened at one end. Reprinted in black-and-white by Belardo (1956). Cf. "Les couleurs pontificales".

56. MacSwiney de Mashanaglass. Pidoux, "Les origines de la cocarde pontificale".

57. Ceresa reports the date from a contemporary diary by Abbot Luca Antonio Benedetti. Loyalist forces are recorded by MacSwiney de Mashanaglass, pp. 11 & 23; and Belardo. Cf. Vigevano, p. 70.

58. MacSwiney de Mashanaglass, p. 12. Zara, pp. 134–135.

59. Pidoux, "Les origines de la cocarde pontificale". MacSwiney de Mashanaglass.

60. Letter of Major Bonfigli to French General Sémaroís, 11 May 1809, quoted in Pidoux, p. 460.

61. *Verzameling* (1834) shows the flag of Papal Ancona as a horizontal bicolor of red over yellow, and *Flaggen-Almanac* (1844) shows the same flag bisected with the tiara and keys; but these designs may date from an earlier era. Red and yellow were the heraldic colors of Ancona from the Middle Ages; cf. Ziggioto, "Le bandiere degli stati italiani", part II, p. 102f.

62. Improbable theories include a flag used by Jerusalem's crusader kings—a gold Jerusalem cross on a white field (cf. Smith, Flags, p. 47). Others appeal to the colors as "heavenly", or argue that popes are exempt from heraldry's rules for artistic visibility—i.e., the rule of "metal and tincture", which specifies that colored emblems ("charges") should contrast with their background; thus a yellow (or gold) emblem should not be charged upon white (or silver). However, since juxtaposing them is not prohibited, the rule is less applicable in the case of two stripes.

63. MacSwiney de Mashanaglass, pp. 13–14. Zara, p. 135. Vigevano, p. 70. Ceresa.

64. Dante Alighieri, *Divine Comedy, Purgatorio*, Canto 9:117–118. Cf. Ziggioto, "La bandiera della marina pontificia di finanza", p. 21.

65. Pietro Perugino (1450–1524), "The Giving of the Keys to St. Peter", Sistine Chapel fresco, Vatican City, ca. 1481.

66. Artaud de Montor, p. 341. Lafond, p. 340. Madelin, p. 21. French sources refer to the "*pavillon pontifical*", which Italian translations render as either "flag" or "arms" (*stemma*).

67. Vigevano, p. 71. Ceresa.

68. Illustration crop from "Particolori dell'equipaggiamento della Guardia Civica dello Stato Pontificio," watercolor on paper showing cockade of yellow surrounded by white, stamped no. 957654, undated, Museo Centrale del Risorgimento Italiano, Rome; reproduced with permission (Istituto per la Storia del Risorgimento Italiano). Illustration of hat from Museo Civico del Risorgimento, Bologna, inventory no. 1328, showing a captain's hat of the Legione Bolognese, 1848/1849; retrieved online (27 June 2018) at: <bbcc.ibc.regione.emilia-romagna. it/pater/loadcard.do?id_card=73755>. Cf. Vigevano, p. 71, and tables portraying uniforms throughout. Piroli consistently shows the colors concentrically rather than juxtaposed—a pattern that gave birth to vulgar epithets dubbing them "toasted eggs" ("uova toste").

69. *Journal de Paris*, 30 May 1814, p. 4. "Agostino Rivarola" [papal legate], *Wikipedia*, retrieved online (18 June 2018) at: <it.wikipedia.org/wiki/Agostino_Rivarola>.

70. Illustration from painting by Christoffer William Eckersberg (1783–1853), "View Across the Tiber towards Castel S. Angelo in Rome", ca. 1815, Statens Museum for Kunst, Copenhagen, Denmark, no. KMS1346, retrieved online (18 June 2018) at: <cspic.smk.dk/ globus/GLOBUS%202006/KMS1346.jpg> with commentary at <www.smk.dk/udforsk-kunsten/soeg-i-smk/#/detail/KMS1346>. Curators report that the top stripe is "red/orange" rather than pure yellow, leaving the composer's intentions uncertain (A. V. Joergensen, email to author, 12 December 2012). The Danish painter studied in Florence and Rome from 1813–1816, and the painting (composed in Rome) is based on a drawing dated 7–8 May 1815; the latter date was the contemporary feast day of the Apparition of St. Michael the Archangel—for whom the fortress was named (which likely explains the festal flag display).

71. Illustration from Brunn-Rasmussen auctioneers, Copenhagen, retrieved online (18 June 2018) at: <www.bruun-rasmussen.dk/img/g/BRFull/Arkiv/Bredgade/795/5002-795.jpg> with explanatory text at: <www.bruun-rasmussen.dk/search.do?mode=detail&iid=3002112 71&tg=classic>. His own reproduction (sold in 2008), composed in Copenhagen, is slightly larger and later (1818) than the original, with minor embellishments.

72. See engraving by Philippe Benoist (ca. 1870), "Pont et Chateau Saint-Ange—Ponte e Castello Sant'Angelo", in Champagny et al., vol. 3, p. 64f (second annexed illustration; the author holds a color version obtained in Rome); and p. 65. A vexillum with Pius's arms at the fort is also shown in an engraving ("La fuga") in Pinto, between p. 146 & 147. The display of two *vexilla* at Castel Sant'Angelo is quite old, and in previous centuries they bore red fields: cf. "Drapeaux pontificaux", p. 98.

73. See pp. 51–57. Relatively clear images of the papal flag atop the fort in the 1800s are surprisingly rare. The author is aware of only two; one here, and another in Fig. 2.22 (along with actual fort flag specimens).

NOTIFICAZIONE

PIER FRANCESCO PER LA MISERICORDIA DI DIO VESCOVO DI ALBANO CARDINALE GALLEFFI, DELLA S.R.C. CAMERLENGO

Essendo la SANTITA' DI NOSTRO SIGNORE PAPA LEONE XII. felicemente regnante venuta nella determinazione di reprimere gli arbitrj usati da alcuni naviganti, e di stabilire l'uniformità nei colori e nelle forme delle Bandiere Pontificie, che si sogliono innalberare dai Legni dello Stato ; ne ha comandato di prescrivere , quanto per oracolo della stessa SANTITA' SUA , e per l'autorità del nostro ufficio di Camerlengato veniamo ad ordinare:

1.° La Bandiera Pontificia , che tutti i Legni dello Stato da commercio , e da pesca dovranno da qui in avanti innalberare , sarà per la metà attaccata all' asta di color giallo , e di color bianco per l'altra metà nel di cui mezzo sarà dipinto il triregno colle chiavi , a norma dei modelli depositati in tutti gli Ufficj di Porto.

2.° La Bandiera da innalberarsi dai Legni addetti al servizio della Finanza sarà della stessa forma e colori, fuorichè in vece del triregno sarà dipinto nella metà bianca il Gonfalone colle chiavi , sopra al quale vi saran poste le lettere iniziali = *Reverenda Camera Apostolica* = , e nella metà di color giallo vi sarà scritto servizio di finanza a norma dei modelli che saranno trasmessi da Monsig. Tesoriere Generale .

3.° I Legni mercantili dello Stato dovranno pure essere forniti di una Bandiera di riconoscimento e per chiedere soccorso , da innalberar si sempre all' albero di maestra , la quale sarà della stessa forma e colori che la prescritta nell' Art. 1.° coll' aggiunta però di una fascia larga di color rosso intorno all' estremità della medesima , fuorchè in quella che sta attaccata all' asta.

4.° La dimensione e ampiezza di tali Bandiere saranno determinate da ciascun Proprietario secondo la grandezza e portata dei Legni.

5.° I Legni a poppa quadra , e matati d coffa l'innalbereranno sull' asta , che d'ordinario si colloca a poppa , e tutti gli altri Legni l'innalbereranno sull' albero di maestra .

6.° E' vietato a tutti i Legni sopraddetti d'innalberare sulla cima degli alberi veruna fiamma collo stemma Pontificio , ma potranno essi solamente far uso di una lunga striscia di color bianco e senza stemma.

7.° In ciascun giorno festivo di precetto , ogni Legno Pontificio stanziato nei Porti dello Stato o Esteri , sarà obbligato di tenere innalberata la suddetta Bandiera dal levare al tramontare del Sole , qualora non lo impedisse un vento gagliardo e burrascoso .

8.° Tutti i Proprietarj de' Legni da commercio saranno tenuti di fornirsi delle sopraindicate Bandiere dentro il termine di mesi quattro , e quelli de' Legni da pesca dentro il termine di mesi due da computarsi dalla pubblicazione della presente Notificazione .

9.° Chiunque dentro il prescritto termine non avrà provveduto il suo Legno delle ordinate Bandiere , o in appresso per colpevole negligenza ne mancasse , sarà punito col ritiro del passaporto marittimo.

10.° Quelli poi i quali si permettessero in avvenire di cambiare in qualche modo le forme , e colori prescritti negli articoli 1.° 2.° 3.° e 6.° saranno puniti colla multa non minore di scudi dieci , e non maggiore di scudi trenta .

11.° Monsig. Tesoriere Generale per la parte che riguarda i Legni di Finanza , gl' Ispettori e Uffiziali di Porto dello Stato , e i Consoli , Vice-Consoli , e Agenti Consolari Pontificj residenti ne' Porti Esteri restano rispettivamente incaricati della osservanza delle presenti disposizioni .

Dato in Camera Apostolica il 17. Settembre 1825.

P. F. Card. Galleffi Camerlengo di S. Chiesa.

G. Groppelli Uditore.

Gioacchino Maria Farinetti Se,r. e Cane. della R. C. A.

ROMA 1825 Presso Vincenzo Poggioli Stampatore Camerale

Figure 2.1. Government Notification, 1825, Papal States Maritime Ensigns

Chapter 2
The Rise of Yellow-White Flags (1825–1870)

Yellow-White Ensigns

 After Pius VII adopted a yellow-white cockade in 1808, many papal flags changed within a generation. His successor introduced new maritime ensigns, and in time new military colors and fort flags arose as well.

For several centuries Papal States flags had borne white fields like those of the French ancien régime. After the French revolution and its attendant expansionism under the *Tricolore*, however, many continental European flags changed. Flags with stripes, both vertical and horizontal, appeared more often, especially in tricolor form. Indeed France twice occupied Italy (including the Papal States) and introduced various tricolor flags for a time.

Pontifical authorities under Leo XII first introduced striped papal flags for a suite of maritime ensigns in 1825. The flags featured the yellow-white colors of the cockade of his predecessor, and took the form of a vertical "bicolor"— a flag with two stripes rather than three. By the fall of papal Rome in 1870, nearly all papal flags of note used the same core pattern (see Appendices I & II).

The 1825 flags now regularized the civil ensign for papal merchant ships, which had often flown the white war ensign to feign armed might and ward off pirates. Similar situations obtained elsewhere. Like its counterparts in Europe, the papal government now sought to standardize its civil ensign in light of new international agreements that ended North African piracy, agreements that followed the fall of Algiers to European forces in 1816.[1]

The new papal flags comprised a civil ensign, state ensign, and pilot ensign, as stipulated in a "Notification" of 17 September 1825 by Pierfrancesco Galleffi,[2] the cardinal chamberlain (*camerlengo*) who oversaw matters of trade and finance (Fig. 2.1 and Appendix IV). Though no actual flag specimens appear to survive,

Bandiera per i Legni da Commercio e da Pesca

Figure 2.2. Civil Ensign, 1825 official model

Rome's Biblioteca Casanatense preserves the original Notification and accompanying "models", color drawings to guide flagmakers (Figs. 2.2 & 2.4–5).[3] Illustrations also appear in previously-mentioned books or manuscripts of the era, including an undated annex to the 1819 *Pavillons,* the 1834 *Verzameling* dispatches, the Papal States *Quadro,* and the 1858 book by LeGras.

The decree states in part:

> NOTIFICATION [by] Cardinal Pier Francesco Galleffi, Bishop of Albano, … Chamberlain of the H[oly] R[oman] C[hurch] …
>
> Pope Leo XII … having come to the determination of repressing the arbitrary [things] used by some navigators, and of establishing uniformity in the colors and forms of the Papal Flags which are ... hoisted by [Papal] State[s] Ships, has commanded ...
>
> 1st: The Papal Flag which all State commerce and fishing ships must hereafter hoist will be of yellow color for the half attached to the mast, and of white color for the other half in the center of which will be depicted the tiara with the keys, according to the norm of the models deposited in all Port Offices.
>
> 2nd: The Flag to be hoisted by Ships attached to the Treasury Service will be of the same form and colors, except that instead of the tiara [there] will be depicted in the white half the Gonfalon with the keys, above which will be placed the initial letters—Reverenda Camera Apostolica [Reverend Apostolic Chamber]—and in the yellow half will be inscribed Servizio di Finanza according to the norm of the models which will be forwarded by the Monsignor Treasurer-General.
>
> 3rd: Merchant Ships of the State must furthermore be furnished with a Flag of recognition and to request aid, always to be hoisted at the mainmast, which will be of the same form and colors as that prescribed in the 1st Art. with the addition, however, of a large band of red color around the extremity of the same, excluding that which is attached to the mast.

Figure 2.3. Civil Ensign, 1858 illustration

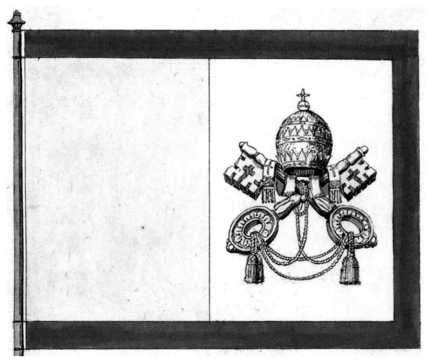

Figure 2.4. Pilot Ensign, 1825 official model (detail)

4th: The dimensions and expanse of such Flags will be determined by each Owner according to the size and capacity of the Ships.

5th: The Ships [so furnished] at the stern ... will raise it[/them] on the mast, ... and all the other Ships will hoist it/[them] on the main-mast.

6th: It is prohibited to all above-mentioned Ships to hoist on the peak of the masts any streamer with the Papal arms, but … only … to make use of a long streamer of white color and without arms.

7th: On each holy day of obligation, every Papal Ship stationed in State or foreign ports will be obliged to have hoisted the above-mentioned Flag from the rising of the sun to [its] setting, unless it is impeded by a vigorous and stormy wind.

8th: All commerce ship Owners will have to furnish themselves with the above-mentioned Flags within … four months, and those which are fishing Ships within … two months ….[4]

The official 1825 model for the civil ensign is annotated, "Flag for Merchant and Fishing Ships" (Fig. 2.2).[5] An 1858 LeGras image provides a comparison (Fig. 2.3).[6] Essentially the new design transformed a former white civil ensign variant (with the tiara-and-keys emblem—see Fig. 1.14) into a bicolor format. The new design is noteworthy because after the Papal States fell in 1870, Vatican City State resurrected it in 1929 as its state flag— a choice to be examined later.[7] The design also served as the basis for the Papal States pilot ensign which bore a red border on three sides (Fig. 2.4), and sometimes all four.[8]

The state ensign for customs vessels bore the papal keys beneath the ceremonial umbrella signifying the Roman Church and its temporal power (Figs. 2.5–6).[9] The latter was associated with the cardinal-chamberlain (*camerlengo*) who oversaw the state treasury. Artwork features the state ensign as early as 1830 (Fig. 2.7).[10] Flag books also report that these vessels flew a long masthead streamer that was yellow at the hoist and white at the fly, with the umbrella-and-keys emblem disposed vertically at the onset of the white (see Fig. 1.3, no. 10).[11] As a coast guard, the customs fleet absorbed the navy in 1856,[12] but whether

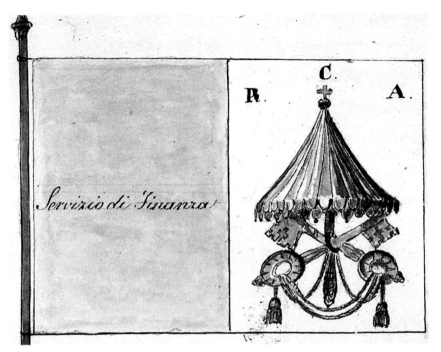

Figure 2.5. State Ensign, official model (detail), 1825

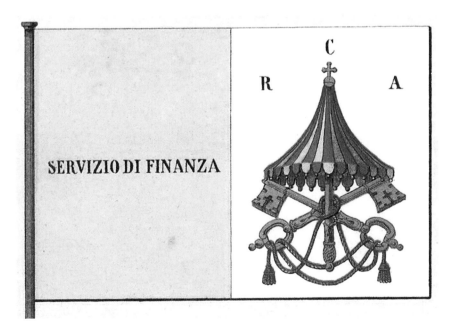

Figure 2.6. State Ensign, 1858 illustration

flag usage changed is unclear. Though captions are lacking for the government chart *Quadro* (issued between 1855 and 1870), it shows naval ensigns verified by actual flag specimens, as well as (presumably) a modified state ensign, with initials but without inscriptions or streamer (see Fig. 1.4, no. 8).[13]

A later decree (8 January 1855) created two award flags for distinguished merchant marine captains, featuring yellow-and-white fields with effigies of Ss. Peter and Paul. These re-fashioned the war ensign design in bicolor format. The first-class award was a bicolor bordered in red, with St. Paul on the yellow stripe and St. Peter on the white, each on a grassy mound; the second-class award had a white field bearing the apostles, and bordered in yellow (Fig. 2.8; also see Fig. 1.4, nos. 9–10; and Appendix IV).[14]

A few years after the 1825 decree, the yellow-white papal colors were clearly employed in land-based flags, to be treated presently. The first known examples are the flags of the Papal Infantry and the Civic Guard.

Infantry Colors

By the 19th century European military regiments generally carried two flags. The lesser one represented the unit itself and its fighting traditions. The other was more significant: it was the sovereign's flag and usually bore his colors or coat of arms.[15] In many countries this was called "the King's color" to honor the monarch, or "the Colonel's color" in recognition of the officer whose company carried it, or the "national color" in republics, but in the Papal States it was called "the papal flag".

In the 18th century the papal infantry color was often white with the pope's personal arms and other adornments.[16] These flags are reasonably well-attested by various archival sources. For 19th-century flags, a significant resource is the Piroli Collection—a compilation of watercolors showing Roman military uniforms and flags from 1823 to 1870.

The first 19th-century infantry color is shown in watercolors dated 1826 and 1827, sometimes bearing anachronistic arms. The flag was white with the pontiff's arms in the center, surmounted by the tiara-and-keys emblem and framed by a green wreath (Fig. 2.9).[17] The square field was fringed in gold, and bore a single gold frame-border (which sometimes appears reddish) set

Figure 2.7. State Ensign, 1830, Papal Coast Guard vessel

Figure 2.8. Award Ensigns, 1855–1870

Figure 2.9. *Infantry Color, 1826*
Grenadier, Leo XII

Figure 2.10. *Infantry color, 1835*
Grenadier, Gregory XVI

slightly inside the white edges of the flag. Gold six-pointed stars adorned each corner. The staff was spirally red and yellow, and bore golden cords and tassels with a silver lance-head. The basic design likely dates from the pontificate of Pius VII (1800–1823); and since the new papal colors of gold and white are prominent, it was likely created after their adoption (1808) and the restoration of the Papal States (1814–15).

Under Gregory XVI the papal infantry adopted flags with yellow and white stripes disposed diagonally (Fig. 2.10)[18]—a pattern akin to French regiments of the era.[19] The Piroli Collection first attested diagonal bicolors in 1831 for Rome's Civic Guard, a home militia whose flags are treated later. The infantry likely received theirs at the same time, though first attested by Piroli in 1832. The flag was square and divided diagonally from upper hoist to lower fly, with yellow at the hoist and white at the fly. The stripes were bisected by a red disk bearing a tiara-and-keys emblem (with both keys in gold). The disk was encircled by a white border inscribed in black GREGORIO XVI P.O.M. Its edge was trimmed in black, with rounded serrations. The flagstaff was yellow with

Figure 2.11. Infantry Color, 1846–1849, 2nd Foreign Regiment, Pius IX

Figure 2.12. Infantry Color, 1860, 2nd Foreign Regiment, Pius IX

a lance-head finial, and bore a cravat with two tails, one yellow and one white. Each tail had fringe and bore the tiara-and-keys emblem in miniature toward the bottom—in gold on the white tail and in silver on the yellow one. The fringe on the flag is usually shown as gold, but in one instance is silver along the bottom hem; the lance-head is usually gold, but in one instance silver.

Gregory's successor, Pius IX, initially authorized the same design, as attested by two infantry colors preserved in Switzerland. One is held by the Nidwalden Museum in Stans (Fig. 2.11), and the other by the Valerian Museum in Sion (Sitten). Both are identified as the "color of the 2nd foreign regiment in service to the Papal States 1846–1849".[20] They bear inscriptions honoring Pius in his reign's first year (PIO IX – P.O.M. – ANNO I). Both keys are golden-yellow, bound by a cord of the same color. The flags have golden-yellow fringe, and bear a three-tailed cravat in the Italian colors: one green, one white, and one red, each with gold fringe.

The cravat recalls Pius's initial empathy for rising pan-Italian nationalism and the Risorgimento. Indeed, early in his reign, pan-Italian sentiments galvanized around him as he pursued political reforms—culminating in the first Papal States constitution on 14 March 1848.[21] In consequence, on 18 March the interior minister, Gaetano Recchi, issued a decree that "the white-yellow papal flag will be adorned by a cravat of the Italian colors." The decree apparently referred to military colors alone and was followed two days later by a corresponding order from the defense minister.[22]

Shortly thereafter the papal flag bearing the pan-Italian cravat was carried by papal troops commanded by Piedmontese General Giovanni Durando.[23] The detachment was sent to lend moral support to Piedmont amid tension with Austria, whose empire held Italy's northeast. Indeed, Swiss troops serving Pius's detachment during the Battle of Vicenza waved their papal flags at Durando's lodging—presumably the two infantry flags preserved today in Switzerland.[24] Elsewhere other unofficial flags of various designs were carried as auguries of papal favor.[25]

Because Pius resisted actual war against Catholic Austria, he suffered politically and a republican revolution ensued. He fled Rome for Gaeta in November 1848. The revolution collapsed in 1849 as armies from France and Austria invaded the Papal States and restored papal authority on 15 July. The French stayed on to protect the pope's claim to Rome and the Austrians stayed to protect his jurisdiction over the outlying provinces. Pius returned to Rome on 12

Figure 2.13. Infantry Color, 1862–1870, contemporary photo

April 1850, residing from then on at the Vatican (a religious center) instead of the Quirinal Palace (the seat of civil government).

Sometime after the Papal States restoration, a new infantry color was introduced without the tricolor cravat, probably upon restructuring from 1849 to June 1852 (when new finials are recorded).[26] It lasted until 1860 and was carried by papal forces against Piedmont's pan-Italian army at Perugia, Pesaro, San Angelo, Ancona, and Castelfidardo. All flag specimens were lost or destroyed in battle, except for one captured by Piedmontese forces at the Battle of Castelfidardo on 18 September 1860, and now held by the Royal Armory of Turin (Fig. 2.12).[27]

The vertical bicolor is surmounted by a red roundel, charged with Pius's coat of arms supported by the tiara and keys. Circling the red roundel is a golden inscription with the regiment's name: FANTERIA DI LINEA SECONDO REGGIMENTO ESTERO. Its ornamental laurel branches are silver on the yellow stripe and gold on the white stripe; the fringe is gold. Its pole bears a

Figure 2.14. Hand-tinted version of photo in Figure 2.13 (detail; undated)

lancehead finial from which hangs a single remaining yellow cord with a tassel (the other is lost).

On 3 May 1862 the final papal infantry color was blessed by Pius IX and presented to commanders at Anzio.[28] It was a plain yellow-white vertical bicolor with no emblem or inscription, and was adorned with gold fringe as well as a fringed cravat composed of two yellow-white tails.[29] It was carried on several campaigns, including the Battle of Mentana in 1867, and served until Italy seized papal Rome in 1870. Its simple design reflected the decisive core pattern for bicolor papal flags in place by the time of the Papal States' demise.

Although no specimen is known to have survived, three contemporary sources confirm its design: a photo from the 1860s, held by Rome's Archivio Fotografico Comunale, depicting a tableau of papal troops, one of whom holds the color (Figs. 2.13–14);[30] a painting of the Battle of Mentana held by the Vatican (1868);[31] and a color lithograph in a memoir by Baron de Charette, a Papal Zouave veteran (Fig. 2.15, ca. 1877).[32] Further confirmation is found in

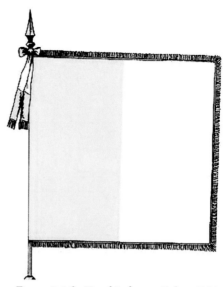

Figure 2.15. Final Infantry Color, lithograph, ca. 1877

Figure 2.16. Final Infantry Color, 1920 illustration

Figure 2.17. Final Infantry Color, 1918 watercolor, detail of color-bearers: Line Infantry (left) & Papal Zouaves (right)

two papal military retrospectives: one by the official Italian military historian (Fig. 2.16, 1920);[33] and one by a papal nobleman, featuring dual watercolors showing the regimental flag-bearers of the line infantry and the Papal Zouaves (Fig. 2.17, ca. 1918).[34] The flag also appears in commemorative artwork by Lionel Royer, a Zouave protégé of Charette.[35]

The Papal Zouaves (*Les Zouaves Pontificaux*) were light infantrymen whose name and uniform derived from Algeria in the 1830s. Formed on 1 January 1861 from a battalion of Franco-Belgian volunteers who fought at Castelfidardo, the Zouaves became a full regiment with recruits from many lands. In 1870 their infantry color was saved from capture by Captain Auguste de Fumel, who hid it within his uniform. Later it was shredded by Charette and distributed among the officers as a talisman for their return home. These fragments are preserved by Zouave descendants today.[36]

Other Zouave flags include a small fanion replica held by the Royal Museum of the Army in Brussels (Fig. 2.18), which also holds a photo of the original.[37] It is white with a yellow border and Pius's arms in the center. The tiara-and-keys emblem is embroidered in silver; the arms are highlighted in yellow. The reverse is plain yellow, and its frayed edges show traces of fringe. Pius presented it to the Zouaves' predecessors, a battalion of Franco-Belgian Papal Sharpshooters, who carried it in 1860 at the Battle of Castelfidardo. Pius received another flag in tribute to the Zouaves from some U.S. matrons in 1867; he gave it to the unit on 5 May 1868 (Fig. 2.19). The bicolor is bisected with his arms and adorned with honorary inscriptions and a battle honor recalling their heroism at Castelfidardo.[38]

The Papal Zouaves were a brainchild of the papal army commander, Christophe de Lamoricière. A faded fanion of his squadron staff at Castelfidardo in 1860 was a unique vertical bicolor, with white at the hoist and yellow at the fly (Fig. 2.20).[39] The obverse was bisected by Pius's arms; the reverse bore the general's arms (above those of four guides). A bicolor cravat (divided lengthwise) also bore these two arms.

Devotees worldwide preserve artifacts or reenact the exploits of foreign papal volunteers. The Irish "Battalion of St. Patrick" had a green gonfalon with St. Patrick's image on the obverse, the Madonna's image on the reverse, and gold inscriptions.[40] Dutch Zouaves had an elaborate gonfalon with St. Michael's image.[41] Flemish Zouave veterans had a vertical bicolor bisected by Pius's arms.[42]

Figure 2.18.   Fanion replica: Franco-Belgian Sharpshooters

Figure 2.19.   Zouaves Tribute Flag, 1867–8: from U.S. Matrons

Figure 2.20. Fanion, 1860: Lamoricière Squadron Staff Guides (arms of Pius IX, obverse of faded white-and-yellow flag)

In Montreal, French-Canadian Zouave recruits received a white flag in 1868. The obverse bore a tiara-and-keys emblem; the reverse bore a unit badge featuring a beaver, maple leaves, and the Zouave motto. After arriving in Rome, the field was altered to yellow-white stripes;[43] but the dual central emblems likely remained—thus bisecting the stripes, as in an old veterans' flag.[44] Hence one side was a yellow-white vertical bicolor bisected by a tiara-and-keys emblem.

This flag pattern also appears in a painting by Marius Richard (1887) at the Vatican Historical Museum, honoring France's loyalty to the papacy.[45] In it a fallen Zouave holds a vertical bicolor bisected by a tiara-and-keys emblem in gold; the staff bears a yellow-white cravat. French Zouave descendants carry a similar flag today.[46] Though unconfirmed as a military color, this flag did serve as a papal fort flag.

Fort, Civil, and State Flags

Further yellow-white papal flags were flown in the Papal States at private palaces and forts. These included key fortified garrison sites in each city (termed "fort flags" or "war flags"), and "civil flags" for popular display. These bicolor

Figure 2.21a. Fort flag, 1870

Figure 2.21b. Fort flag, 1870, detail (reverse)

flags were inspired by yellow-and-white military colors used ashore under Gregory XVI and Pius IX, which in turn evolved from bicolor ensigns at sea under Leo XII (see Appendices I & II). Apparently the new fort and civil flags lacked uniformity or legal codification, but were commonly recognized as legitimate. Simple and distinctive, they rivaled Italy's tricolor during the Risorgimento, especially under Pius IX, who struggled to preserve the Papal States.

Two fort flags from Rome (1870) are still preserved. The first is a vertical bicolor composed of six vertical breadths of wool (three yellow, three white) bisected by a tiara-and-keys emblem. The latter is embroidered, and comprises a white tiara, with colored jewels along its crowns, above two orange-yellow keys bound together by a red cincture; its height is one-third of the flag's width (Fig. 2.21).[47] It was given to the Vatican Gendarmerie in 2011 by Prince Sforza Ruspoli, a descendant of papal nobility.[48] He asserts that this fort flag (*bandiera da fortezza*) flew near Rome's Porta Pia on 20 September 1870. Nearby an army of the Kingdom of Italy breached the city walls and Rome surrendered. The flag was taken for safekeeping to the Villa Bonaparte owned by Cristina Ruspoli, whose descendants preserved it.[49] (The flag's heading bears a cord that is attached to a blue wooden staff, likely for display from a fixed bracket.[50])

The same design also appears in a contemporary Spanish illustration of Rome's surrender,[51] and likely flew at forts elsewhere in 1870. Thus an Italian soldier reported a "white and yellow flag with the gold keys" atop a fort in Civita Castellana at its capture.[52] As early as 1849, a journalist reported it (or a similar flag) at Rome's Castel Sant'Angelo fortress, when French forces deposed the Roman Republic, restored the Papal States, and ceremoniously re-hoisted "the yellow and white banner, emblazoned with the keys of St. Peter",[53] upon appeals from papal authorities.[54] In 1866, when the French departed that fort, a correspondent reported it again: "the French tri-color was hauled down … and the Papal flag, white and yellow, with the cross [sic] keys, unfurled in its stead."[55] Another journalist's sketch of the ceremony likely records it atop the fort, too (Fig. 2.22).[56]

However a second (and different) fort flag flew at Castel Sant'Angelo in 1870: a plain vertical bicolor with no emblem. Held by the Vatican Historical Museum, each stripe comprises three vertically-conjoined breadths of wool (Fig. 2.23).[57] Nearly square, its design corresponds to the infantry color of the era. Lowered upon the fort's surrender to Italian forces on 21 September, it was taken by a *bersagliere* from Genoa,[58] and then preserved by a papal

Figure 2.22. French depart Castel Sant'Angelo, 1866; Detail below

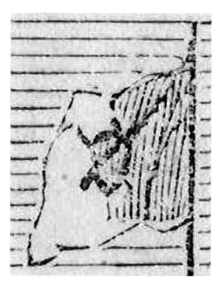

Detail of papal flag atop Castel Sant'Angelo, 1866

Figure 2.23. Fort flag, 1870 (plain bicolor in backgound)

chamberlain; his daughter's descendants, the Boggiano Pico family, gave it to John Paul II in Genoa in 1985.[59]

The variance between this flag (without an emblem) and the Ruspoli design (which bears one), suggests that no uniform fort flag existed. Fortress protocols are silent on the matter,[60] and detailed eyewitness descriptions are rare.[61] It may be that precise standardization never evolved, and perhaps further variations existed.[62] We cannot be certain unless future discoveries are made.

Likewise uncertain is precisely when bicolor fort flags replaced traditional white designs (Fig. 2.24). The LeGras book (1858) records only a white fort flag bearing the pope's personal arms (which at times was replaced by the tiara-and-keys emblem alone; see Figs. 1.12–15).[63] But this is incomplete; for by mid-century, bicolors were gradually replacing white designs—though in disparate

Figure 2.24.   Fort flags (variety), Pius IX

Figure 2.25.   Undated painting of civil flags (detail): Pius IX in the Piazza del Popolo, 1846

fashion. From 1846 through 1848, white fort flags are depicted in Rome, Civitavecchia, Bologna,[64] and Civita Castellana.[65] In July 1849, however, an official reported a "white and yellow" fort flag at Rome, despite a "white" one at Civitavecchia; other reports in 1849 confirm bicolors at Rome.[66] Forts elsewhere flew bicolors over time, as recorded at Civitavecchia (1862),[67] Porto d'Anzio (1862),[68] and Civita Castellana (1870).[69]

Thus, by 1849 bicolor fort flags clearly replaced white ones in Rome, but elsewhere only later. Indeed the trend may have begun as early as 1815, but this is otherwise unconfirmed, and thus uncertain (see Figs. 1.30–31). In any case, by 1870, all forts likely flew bicolors, especially after the Papal States were reduced to Lazio (1860).[70] They likely bore vertical stripes after Pius IX was restored, as typified by other bicolors of that period (see Appendices I & II).[71] The Ruspoli design was likely preferred: it comprised the simpler white fort flag (i.e., with a tiara-and-keys emblem alone) in bicolor format. It seems the best attested at forts, was used by Papal Zouave veterans and devotees,[72] and served as a proto-national papal flag after 1870. Flags of this period are described later.[73]

Papal civil flags for unofficial, popular use were likewise diverse. These festoon streets and buildings in two paintings of Roman scenes under Pius IX. One is undated but contemporary (Fig. 2.25); and the other dates from 1877.[74] Such flags are well-attested on public occasions by eyewitnesses and historians, who report that yellow-white flags "were used in civil ceremonies to decorate streets in the pontifical colors."[75] The preferred version was likely a plain bicolor—whether vertical (likely inspired by France's tricolor) or horizontal (likely inspired by Austria's Hapsburg bicolor, i.e., black over yellow).[76]

Other civil flag patterns are also documented. A small, yellow-white flag divided quarterly is held by the Museo Civico del Risorgimento in Modena,[77] while diagonal bicolors appear in an 1846 sketch recalling a railway inauguration. The latter pattern recalls an infantry color of the era, and the bicolors bear various charges, such as the tiara-and-keys emblem or honorary inscriptions.[78]

When these civil flags originated is unclear. Perhaps they were known by 1834, when a flag chart identified a plain vertical bicolor (with no emblem) as a "Signal flag for communication with shore interests" (Fig. 2.26).[79] The meaning is unclear, but it was probably semi-official. After 1870 plain bicolors endured as unofficial papal flags in Italy and elsewhere—as also today (to be examined later).[80]

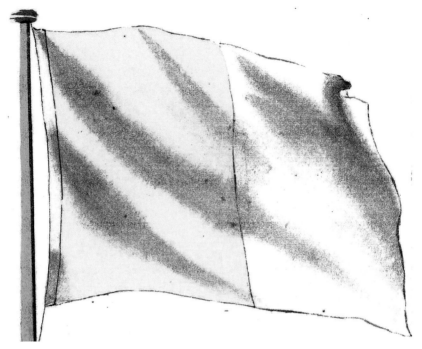

Figure 2.26. "Signal Flag", 1834

Figure 2.27. State flag, 1900, Argentine papal legation

While fort and civil flags were common, state flags (flags appointed for state offices) cannot be found. Perhaps none existed, and absent clear evidence, presuming their use would be anachronistic. No papal act prescribed the custom, which was still evolving in Europe as state buildings began flying their nation's fort flag.[81] At times papal state agents were stationed in protected garrison zones flying a fort flag anyway;[82] or at the Quirinal Palace, a papal residence and seat of civil government, the Swiss Guard flag (see Fig. 1.24). By contrast, plaques bearing papal arms are common at state offices (unlike flags). Perhaps they flew civil flags whenever area buildings did likewise, but state flags cannot be ruled out in some sense. Some diplomatic posts likely flew them before 1870, as they did afterward; e.g., Argentina's papal legation flew the Ruspoli design (1900, Fig. 2.27).[83] More on this later.[84]

As the preceding survey of diverse flags on land further shows, the term "papal flag" evoked a symbolic principle (papal sovereignty) but not a uniform design. Standardized national flags are taken for granted by observers today; but in the Papal States and elsewhere, designs on land were less strictly codified than those at sea. Still, however catalyzed and endorsed, each flag embodied familiar papal symbolism and was readily identified as a "papal flag".

Civic and Palatine Guard

Other papal forces also carried distinctive flags, many of which were yellow-white bicolors. These included the ceremonial colors of the Civic Guard and the Palatine Honor Guard, as well as those of the civic districts of Rome.

The Civic Guard was a home militia in various Papal States cities—similar to those in other Italian states. In Rome under Pius VII, its initial flag was reportedly blue upon reconstitution in 1815. In 1823 under Leo XII it appears thus in a Piroli Collection watercolor, with his arms (surrounded by a green wreath and surmounted by the tiara-and-keys) and a golden-yellow frame-border set slightly inside the hem, a pattern reminiscent of the white infantry flag of the era. The border is followed by a pattern of interlaced ovals of the same color, and six-pointed stars. The flag has gold fringe and golden cords and tassels attached to the staff, which is red with yellow spikes, all surmounted by a golden statuette of St. Michael the Archangel. In 1829 the same flag appears, but with the arms of Pius VIII. The golden-frame border is omitted, and the finial is a silver lance-head (Fig. 2.28).[85]

Figure 2.28. Civic Guard color, 1829, Pius VIII

Figure 2.29. Civic Guard color, 1831, Gregory XVI

Figure 2.30a. Civic Guard color (obverse), 1846, Pius IX

Figure 2.30b. Civic Guard color (reverse), 1846, Pius IX

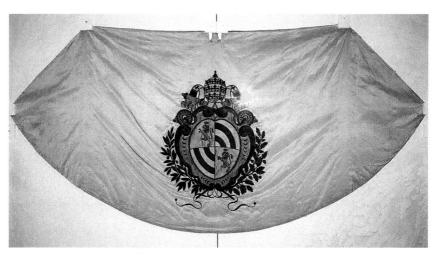

Figure 2.31. Civic Guard labarum, 1847, Pius IX

In 1831 under Gregory XVI, the Rome Civic Guard was shown with a new, yellow-white flag (Fig. 2.29)[86]—probably issued at the same time as the infantry, whose earliest yellow-white flag, first attested in 1832, has already been treated. The Guard color was likewise divided diagonally, although in the opposite direction—from upper fly to lower hoist. Otherwise it followed the basic pattern of its predecessors, bearing Gregory's arms within a green wreath and surmounted by the tiara and keys—all surmounting a bicolor with four six-pointed gold stars in the corners. The staff was yellow with a golden lance-head and yellow cords and tassels, and the flag was fringed in gold. It is uncertain how long this flag was used, for by 1841 the Rome Civic Guard was shown carrying the regular infantry flag of the era instead of its own distinctive flag.[87]

The Vatican Historical Museum at the Lateran Palace holds a Rome Civic Guard flag gifted by Bologna, early in the reign of Pius IX (Fig. 2.30).[88] It is quite large and made of white silk. One side bears a black inscription GUAR-DIA CIVICA DI ROMA 1846 in three lines, within a golden wreath of oak; at the corners are olive branches framing the monogram P.IX. The other side bears the arms of Pius IX surmounted by the tiara and keys (one gold and one silver), within a golden wreath of oak and olive branches, with branches also adorning the edges of the flag. The staff's finial bears a circular Roman wreath surmounted by a Christian cross. It also bore a cravat which is not displayed.[89]

Shortly thereafter, Rome's Civic Guard was assigned a white vexillum bearing Pius's personal arms within a wreath above the battalion number in

Figure 2.32. Civic Guard labarum, ca. 1848, Pius IX (detail)

Figure 2.33. Flag-bearer, Bologna Legion, 1848–49 (detail)

Figure 2.34. Flag fragment, Bologna Univ. Battalion, 1848

gold. Its design corresponded to the traditional white fort flag in the form of an unusual labarum. Two specimens from 1847 (or 1848, as sources differ) are held by Rome's Capitoline Museum, and displayed in the Palazzo Senatorio (Fig. 2.31, shown spread out flat).[90] Its central part was curved at the bottom and straight along the top, where it was held by a horizontal crossbar attached to the staff and ornamented with cords and tassels. Its lateral parts hung down in folds on either side and its reverse was plain yellow. Its finial was a Roman eagle within a wreath, standing on a pedestal marked S.P.Q.R. From at least 18 March 1848, its cravat bore tails in the green-white-and-red Italian colors, to reflect the pan-Italian fervor that swept the Papal States, as noted earlier (Fig. 2.32). On May 8 it was carried at the Battle of Cornuda against Austria. The Civic Guard disbanded in 1849 after the Roman Republic collapsed.[91]

Civic Guard units outside Rome had distinctive flags as well. An 1848 watercolor shows a Frascati Civic Guardsman whose rifle bears a fanion; it is yellow over white with a battalion inscription.[92] For Bologna, a contemporary painting shows a guard with a yellow-white vertical bicolor bisected by the arms of Pius IX; the flag bears a cravat and fringe in the Italian colors (Fig. 2.33).[93] A Bologna student battalion had similar flag, but divided horizontally (white over yellow); and a surviving fragment is bisected by Pius's arms on one side, and a battalion inscription on the other, with the date 1848 (Fig. 2.34).[94]

The Palatine Honor Guard Corps was founded by Pius IX in December 1850. It comprised loyal volunteers from the defunct Civic Guard and served

Figure 2.35. Palatine Guard color, 1859–1878, Pius IX

Figure 2.36a. Rome District Flag (obverse), 1847, Pius IX

in the Apostolic Palace, at papal ceremonies, and as a security reserve. In September 1859 it received rights to a flag that was blessed on 31 March 1860. It was reminiscent of the era's infantry color: a vertical yellow-white bicolor with the pontiff's personal arms bisecting the stripes (Fig. 2.35).[95] Both keys are gold, and metallic-gold oak branches frame the flag's corners and arms. Fringe alternating in gold and silver adorned the flag, while a two-tailed cravat (white on one side, yellow on the other) bore golden inscriptions: GUARDIA PALATINA on one tail, D'ONORE on the other. The staff's finial was a golden statuette of St. Michael atop a globe with the motto QUIS UT DEUS?

The Palatine Guard flag was among the few that remained in use after papal Rome collapsed in 1870, because the Corps remained in the pope's service (along with the Swiss Guard, the Noble Guard, and the Gendarmerie). The color was altered with each new pope, whose arms took the place of his predecessor's. Each color is preserved at the Vatican Historical Museum; that of Pius IX is newly restored.[96] Paul VI disbanded the Corps on 14 September 1970—his flag being the last.[97]

Figure 2.36b. Rome District Flag (reverse), 1847, Pius IX

Figure 2.37. Artillery color, 1870, Pius IX

Figure 2.38. Dragoons color, 1870, Pius IX

Yellow-white flags for the fourteen historic *rioni* (civic districts) of Rome were created in 1847 during the reform era that ended in revolution. They are held by the Capitoline Museum in Rome and displayed at the Palazzo Senatorio (examples in Figs. 2.36a and 2.36b).[98] The districts reflected the Civic Guard quarters, and the flags were received when new city councilors were seated on the Capitoline Hill. The silk flags are divided horizontally, white over yellow. An exhibit catalog describes them:

> The edges, adorned with lace, are decorated by silver embroidery of oak branches. Also silver is the embroidered laurel wreath that frames the red-amaranth medallion in which the district's name appears at the center. On the reverse of each is the repeated motif of the [Roman] wolf with the twins [Romulus and Remus]. The [flags] are accompanied by a red ribbon bearing in gold letters the inscription S.P.Q.R. on one side, and PIO IX P.O.M. on the other. The flagstaffs were surmounted by the Roman eagle within a crown of gilded metal with the inscription S.P.Q.R. at the center, surmounted by the name of the Pontiff. On the reverse [of the lance-head appeared] the number of the quarter or of the battalion of the Civic [Guard].[99]

A year later a papal decree reconfirmed that the flags would be carried at civic ceremonies, along with "the vexillum with the inscription S.P.Q.R. [Senatus Populusque Romanum] ... with its standard-bearer".[100]

Other Flags

Several papal forces used flags that were not yellow-white. The flags of the Pontifical Swiss Guards Corps will be treated in the next chapter; the remainder, presently.

The Pontifical Artillery Regiment had a velvet standard, preserved at the Vatican Historical Museum (Fig. 2.37).[101] Disposed vertically from its staff, it was deep blue, and fringed in gold and silver. It was square, and on the obverse bore the arms of Pius IX in the center, accompanied by the golden inscription REGGIMENTO ARTIGLIERIA PONTIFICIA. On the reverse it was simply deep blue. Two golden tassels hung from the bottom corners. It had a deep blue staff and a finial of St. Michael atop a globe.

Figure 2.39. Carabinieri color, Pius VIII

Figure 2.40. Noble Guard color, Gregory XVI

The standard of the Pontifical Dragoons is also preserved at the Vatican Historical Museum (Fig. 2.38).[102] Disposed vertically from its staff, it was dark green velvet, square, and adorned with fringe (and two bottom tassels) of gold and silver. The reverse was plain green; the obverse bore the arms of Pius IX with the keys and tiara, with the inscription DRAGONI PONTIFICI beneath. Its staff was dark green terminating in a spearhead.

The papal police were restructured on 14 July 1816 as the Pontifical Carbineer Corps, and had a green standard highlighted in gold, with the pontiff's arms (Fig. 2.39).[103] After the Roman Republic ended, it was restructured as the *Veliti Pontifici* in 1850, and renamed the Pontifical Gendarme Corps in 1851. Its square flag was dark blue velvet with gold fringe; it bore Pius's arms in the center, above the inscription GENDARMERIA PONTIFICIA. The staff's finial was a statuette of St. Michael atop a globe. Its date of origin is unclear, but it was turned over to Italian forces after the seizure of Papal Rome in 1870. A replica was made under Leo XIII, and the pattern lasted until 1970 (see Fig. 3.45). The final flag is held by the Vatican Historical Museum.[104]

The Pontifical Noble Guard Corps, founded by Pius VII on 11 May 1801, was the pope's mounted guard corps of 77 noblemen. Like the Palatine Honor Guard Corps, it was disbanded in 1970. Its last standard, preserved at the Vatican Historical Museum, followed a traditional pattern established by Pope Pius VII on 31 May 1820 (Fig. 2.40).[105] It was white with the pontiff's arms in the center, a gold border of interlaced ovals, and gold fringe. Trophies of golden weapons appeared at the inner corners, and the name of the corps appeared on the cravat. Later these elements were rearranged a bit.

One member of the Noble Guard was known as the vexillifer or gonfalonier, and carried the *vessillo* or Standard of the Holy Roman Church when the pope traveled in ceremonial processions. In past centuries the vexillifer held an office of considerable repute; and the standard, usually red, had various shapes and designs, as noted previously. In the 19th century, it was a two-tailed, red flag bearing the pope's personal arms surmounted by the tiara-and-keys emblem, and adorned throughout with various golden decorations. The standard used under Pius VII is preserved by the Vatican Historical Museum, and bears an array of golden ornamentations.[106] The latter also appeared in the standard under Gregory XVI, as shown by the Piroli Collection (Fig. 2.41); but under Pius IX the background was arrayed with six-pointed gold stars instead.[107]

1831

VESSILLIFERO E COMANDA

Grantenuta   In gala

Figure 2.41. Vexillifer, 1831, Gregory XVI

The Roman Senate and People also had an honorary flag. It appears often in 19th-century sources, and as early as 1705.[108] It was red with a gold-bordered red shield bearing the gold initials SPQR (*Senatus Populusque Romanus* in Latin). An 1847 decree stated that "the flag of the Roman Senate and People will be hoisted and carried [at] … certain solemn formality[s]."[109] As noted earlier, a similar vexillum accompanied the civic district flags. The SPQR shield, with a cross added to the canton, still serves as the city's coat of arms, and often bisects the modern flag of the Commune of Rome—a vertical bicolor of maroon and gold.[110]

During wartime Castel Sant'Angelo supposedly flew a red flag bearing the image of the Archangel Michael—its patron and namesake—but this is not attested in the 1800s.[111] In any case the final flag at that fort was a white flag of surrender, hoisted on 20 September 1870 after Italian forces breached Rome's walls.[112] Italy's tricolor, bearing the House of Savoy's arms, now flew in Rome.[113]

Summary

A survey of 19th century papal flags yields three conclusions, as shown by the charts in Appendices I & II.

First, papal flags varied; and no specific design became the sole, exclusive "papal flag". That term evoked a symbolic concept (papal sovereignty) more than a uniform design—unlike today's lone, official Vatican flag.

Second, eventually bicolor flag designs dominated the rest—as this chapter shows. These flags recalled the Petrine keys of gold and silver, since in heraldry, gold correlates with yellow, and silver with white. Inspired by a yellow-white cockade that asserted papal independence from Napoleon in 1808, bicolor flags promoted papal sovereignty over and against the secular nationalism associated with Italy's tricolor. In time the new flags largely eclipsed the papacy's older red or white flags (except the navy), refashioning their designs in bicolor format. In this way, yellow and white became the papacy's modern colors.

Third, despite bicolor variations, vertical stripes soon became the dominant papal flag motif—probably when the Papal States were restored in 1849 after a republican revolt. Indeed by 1870, when the Papal States ended, all bicolor flags bore vertical stripes specifically (with or without emblems)—thus reflecting a "core pattern" (Fig. 2.42).

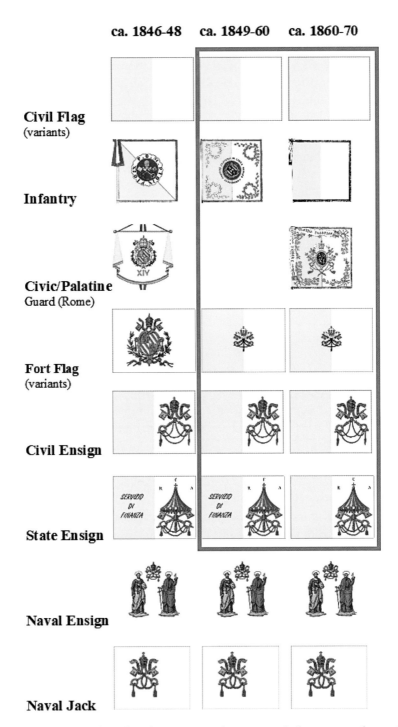

Figure 2.42. Vertical Bicolor Flags, Pius IX: the core Papal Flag pattern after 1849

These trends began largely at sea and spread to land. Vertical bicolors flew at sea from 1825, when Leo XII inaugurated new flags for merchant and customs vessels. Diagonal bicolors flew on land from 1831, when Gregory XVI authorized new flags for the Infantry and Civic Guard. Vertical bicolors replaced these under Pius IX, after the Papal States were restored in 1849—for the Infantry from about 1850, and the Palatine Guard from 1859. At some forts bicolor flags may have flown as early as 1815 (perhaps horizontal), and certainly from 1849 to 1870 (probably vertical); two such specimens survive (both vertical).

Among these designs, three are noteworthy. Each was reviewed in 1929 when the Vatican sought a state flag after reconciling with Italy—and each was a vertical bicolor. The first had no emblem. It served the Papal States as a civil flag (by mid-century) and an infantry color (from 1862), and flew from at least one fort (1870). The second had the tiara-and-keys emblem bisecting the stripes. It flew at some Papal States forts; and after Italy seized Rome, it flew at the Vatican as a proto-national papal flag (from at least 1903).

The third design bore the tiara-and-keys emblem in the fly. It was the civil ensign of the papal merchant marine from 1825 to 1870, when it vanished. But only for a time, for in 1929 this flag was revived by the new Vatican City State. The next chapter will explain that process, including a curious twist of fate: the man who recommended its revival, was the son of the papal commander at Castel Sant'Angelo in 1870, where a papal flag was lowered for the last time.

Notes, Chapter 2

1. Ziggioto, "Le bandiere degli stati italiani", part I, p. 123, n. 28, states that "in that year [1825] the papal flag was 'set free' by the mediation of France, i.e., recognized and no longer disturbed by Algerian privateers", and notes that larger states such as Prussia and Sardinia also had to curb random or whimsical civil ensigns (ibid. n. 27). Cf. Smith, *The Flag Book*, p. 18, regarding France. In an undated, later supplement to its 1819 edition, *Pavillions*, pl. 8-bis, noted that the two white papal civil ensigns had been "suppressed". Cf. also Le Gras, pl. 22, no. 2, regarding the papal war ensign: "merchant ships cannot carry it anymore". Cf. also, Bouquet.

2. Illustration from personal photo of manuscript in author's archives. The text is also found in *Raccolta delle leggi … nello Stato Pontificio*, vol. 9, appendix 1. Cf. also *Bandiere di segnale*, file CS6020 ("Notificazione").

3. Illustrations from *Bandiere di segnale*, files CS6021 ("Bandiera di riconoscimento"), CS6022 ("Bandiera per i Legni da Commercio e da Pesca"), CS6023 ("Bandiera per Servizio di Finanza"); reproduced with permission of Italy's Ministry of Cultural Heritage & Activities. The manuscript collection also includes several pilot ensigns of regional powers to aid port authorities.

4. Galleffi, author's translation. The author could not verify in the papal decrees collection of Rome's Biblioteca Casanatense a supposedly preceding decree of 8 July 1824 reported (likely erroneously) by Vigevano, (p. 72), Ziggioto (part I, pp. 115–116 and *errata corrigere*), Paschini (p. 3), and Holy See Press Office. The decree continues as follows: "9th: Whoever within the prescribed term shall not have provided his Ship with the Flags ordained … will be punished with the withdrawal of their maritime passport. 10th: Those, furthermore, who permit themselves … to change in some way the forms and colors prescribed in articles 1, 2, 3, and 6, will be punished with a fine not less than ten scudi, and not more than thirty scudi. 11th: The Msgr. Treasurer-General for the part which regards the Finance Ships, the Inspectors and Officials of State Port[s], and the Consuls, Vice-Consuls and Papal Consular Agents resident in Foreign Ports, respectively, are charged with the observance of the present dispositions."

5. Illustration from *Bandiere di segnale*, file 006022 ("Bandiera per i Legni da Commercio e da Pesca"). The model illustration is closely followed by *Pavillons*, pl. 8-bis, in an undated supplement, which identifies it as the "ensign for merchant ships and for [those] which [are] fish[ing vessels]."

6. Illustration from Le Gras, plate 22, no. 5, who calls it the "Flag of Fishing Vessels", observing (inaccurately?) that "This ensign is that of fishing ships of the States of the Church. Merchant ships can hoist it on feast days, but only on a particular directive." Its proportions are cited as 3:4.

7. Today's Vatican City constitution similarly provides an "official model" (illustration) for its ceremonial flag, as will be seen. See pp. 95–98.

8. Illustration from *Bandiere di segnale*, file cs006021 ("Bandiera di riconoscimento"). Three sides are likewise red in the post-1819 supplement to *Pavillons*, plate 8-bis, that closely follows the official model and identifies it as the "ensign of recognition for requesting help". Three sides are also red in Le Gras, pl. 22, no. 6, whose citation reads: "Pilot Ensign …. Proportions 3:4 …. All ships of the States of the Church must be furnished with this ensign. It is hoisted at the mainmast to call for a pilot, to appeal for help and to identify oneself, when one navigates on the coastline of the Roman States." Four sides bear the red band in the ensign shown in *Verzameling*, no. 17, and *Quadro*.

9. Illustrations from *Bandiere di segnale*, file 006023 ("Bandiera per Servizio di Finanza"), followed by that of Le Gras, pl. 22, no. 4, who cites proportions of 3:4 and states: "Finance Ensign .... hoisted at the stern of all ships which belong to the service of the administration of finance (customs, etc.). The three letters R.C.A. signify REVERENDA CAMERA APOSTOLICA."

10. Illustration from print of a *Guardacoste pontificio trabaccolo* (two-masted ship) following an Austrian ship, 1830, Museo Navale di Pegli, Genoa. Other artistic attestations include: Ziggioto, "Le bandiere degli stati italiani", part I, p. 123, n. 33 (reference to an 1860 watercolor showing a port scene); and "Naval procession of Pope Gregory XVI from Civitavecchia to Saline Corneto [today Tarquinia]", May 23, 1835, 19th century watercolor, Michele Fonda, Museo di Roma, De Agostini Picture Library via Getty Images, retrieved online (21 June 2018) at <www.gettyimages.com/detail/illustration/naval-procession-of-pope-gregory-xvi-from-civitavecchia-stock-graphic/163236800>.

11. Illustration from LeGras, pl. 22, no. 10. See also *Verzameling*, no. 14. Ziggioto, "La bandiera della marina pontificia di finanza", estimates the ensign's size as about 2 x 2.5 m (6 x 8 ft.), which coincides with existing war ensign specimens; and the streamer about 15 cm x 20 m (6 in. x 66 ft.).

12. Bouquet, p. 73. Alvarez, pp. 44f & 83f. Brandani et al., p. 87f.

13. Lack of a streamer (unlike the war ensign) may suggest use by small or unarmed state vessels. Or its location alongside the Vacant See ensign, might suggest an association of some kind (along with absence of inscriptions). Indeed, the armed steamer *San Pietro* is pictured flying the state ensign in 1848 (Pizutti, cover), but flew the war ensign in 1860 (Fig. 1.18).

14. Giuseppe Milesi, "Notificazione", in "Bandiera Pontificia", Archivio Secreto Vaticano, *Segretaria di Stato*, Anno 1929, Rubr. 240, fasc. 1, ff. 295–296. The text is also found in *Raccolta delle leggi … nello Stato Pontificio*, vol. 9, pp. 1–6. Article 4 specified the designs. Translated by Maury, pp. iv–vii. Cf. also, Le Gras (description only, incorrectly reporting both flags as having a red border); and Ziggioto, "Le bandiere degli stati italiani", part I, p. 119.

15. Wise, p. 20. The author has found no significant evidence of distinctive unit flags to accompany the papal flag in the 1800s.

16. Ales, pp. 75–86, 362–381.

17. Illustration from Piroli, ms. 73/21 (1826 with arms of Leo XII); reproduced with permission (Istituto per la Storia del Risorgimento Italiano). Cf. also ms. 78/57 (1826 with anachronistic arms of Pius VIII), 73/37 (1827 with anachronistic arms of Gregory XVI), 73/38 (1827 with indecipherable arms). Vigevano, p. 72, mistakenly calls the border and stars red. Ales, pp. 86, 382–383 (pl. 106), estimates that the flags were ca. 130 cm (51 in.) square. Piroli, ms. 79/18 (1832), also attests a white flag with golden horns in the corners used early in the reign of Gregory XVI by Cacciatori in Romagna who were named "Zamboni" for their commander; cf. Ales, pp. 87, 384–385 (pl. 107), who changes the flag's oblong orientation to a square.

18. Illustration from Piroli, ms. 73/102 (1835); reproduced with permission (Istituto per la Storia del Risorgimento Italiano). The flag also appears in ibid. ms. 74/15 (1832 *Cacciatore*), with *Granatieri* in mss. 73/99 (1835 and showing silver fringe at the bottom, and gold fringe on the top and side hems), 78/76 (1836), 79/25 (1841), 73/117 (1842); the latter two showing yellow-white alternating fringe. Cf. Vigevano, pp. 73–74; Zara, p. 137; and Ales, pp. 87, 139, and 384–385 (pl. 107, where he mistakenly portrays the flag with a separate reverse, confusing it with a distinct flag used by the Civic Guard early in Gregory's reign), who estimates the flags' size as about 90 cm (35 in.) square, which seems too small in light of existing flag specimens of the same design under Pius IX.

19. Bruckner, pp. 313–314.

20. Illustration from Bruckner, pl. 70; cf. also p. 155. Nidwalden Museum, Stans (identified by Bruckner as the Rathaus, Stans): Christoph Baumgartner, Staatsarchiv Nidwalden, email and photo to author, 20 April 2009. Valerian Museum, Sion: Muriel Pozzi-Escot, Musées cantonaux du Valais, emails and photo to author, 6 April 2009.

21. Cf. *Atti del Sommo Pontifice Pio IX.* It does not reference flags.

22. Decrees in *Gazzetta di Roma*, 20 March 1848, p. 1; reproduced by Vigevano, pp. 71 & 74–75, n. 4. Cf. *Raccolta delle leggi … nello Stato Pontificio*, vol. 2, p. 52. Kertzer, *The Pope who would be King*, p. 60, reports some cravats in use as early as January. Pizutti says the cravat adorned the state ensign, as shown by an undated painting; but the author has yet to confirm this.

23. Rangoni-Machiavelli, p. 76. *Roma 1846–1849*, p. 39, states that the exercise was "composed of two divisions, one regular, and one of volunteers.... The representation of the Civic Guards was numerous...."

24. Ghisi, p. 235. *Pace* Vigevano, pp. 74–75, who mistakenly describes them as *vertical* yellow-white bicolors, with a red central disk bearing Pius' arms.

25. Cf. Ghisi, pp. 233–234, describes a ceremony in which new flags were carried by pan-Italian partisans to be blessed by Pius in advance of a campaign. He also describes a vertical bicolor of white over yellow with a red cross throughout on one side, and Pius' name on the other, preserved today at the Museo del Risorgimento in Ferrara. Still other augury-flags were based on the Italian tricolor.

26. Ales, p. 88: the new flag probably arose in connection with the restructuring of the papal army after the restoration. Vigevano, pp. 1–5, and Alvarez, pp. 72–73, indicate that this took place between August 1849 and 1 June 1852. Chigi, 11 June 1852 entry, notes that a statuette of St. Michael the Archangel was added to the (already existing?) flags of (some?) papal troops (*truppa pontificia*) that day; but statuettes seem attested at this point only for the Artillery and Gendarmeria. Cf. Rangoni-Machiavelli, p. 76.

27. Illustration from Fiora, fig. 77; cf. also p. 105. Vigevano, p. 75, describes the two cords as one white and one yellow. Colangeli, fig. 51 and p. 180. Brandani et al, pp. 90–91, mistakenly omits the tiara-and-keys emblem; as does Ales, pp. 88, 390–391 (pl. 110), though he includes it in his description. Both show the finial as a lance-head, and Ales shows both cords as yellow. Ales shows a silver and gold inscription, but describes it only as gold, which seems to match Fiora.

28. Charette, pp. 19–20, reports the papal speech relating the blessing to the Feast of the Finding of the Holy Cross (May 3). *Civiltà Cattolica*, anno 13, vol. 2, p. 484. Bittard des Portes, pp. 58f, 240 (note the hymn as well). D'Albiousse, pp. 53–56. Bonetti, p. 181. Le Chauf de Kerguenec, pp. 266–268. Innocenti, p. 43. Brandani et al, p. 90. Cf. Gregoverius, p. 155. A long-distance photo of the ceremony is held by the Valenziani collection of the Gabinetto Fotografico Nazionale in Rome ("[Antonio] D'Alessandri—Pio IX consegna le nuove bandiere all'esercito pontificio durante il campo di Anzio, Anzio [Roma] 3 Maggio 1862, da negativo al collodio, Inv F30693"), retrieved online (21 June 2018) at: <www.iccd.beniculturali.it/getImage.php?id=1591&f=0&.jpg> and <www.iccd.beniculturali.it/index.php?it/194/fondi-fotografici/50/valenziani>.

29. Sources differ as to the precise composition of the cravat. Some show one tail in each color; others show each tail as bicolored, either vertically or horizontally.

30. Illustration (black & white) from *Rome in Early Photographs*, pl. 161 (noted as held by the

Archivio Fotografico Comunale, Rome). Illustration (color) from hand-tinted version in author's archives, by G. Agustini Ottico (uncertain date). Cf. Brandani et al., frontpiece. The tableau shows (left to right): above, a Swiss Guard, a Noble Guard, a Palatine Guard (holding the color), a Papal Gendarme; below, an artilleryman, a customs officer, a line infantryman, a Zouave, a chasseur, a firefighter, and a dragoon.

31. Painting by Jacques-Émile Lafon, "La Battaglia di Mentana", oil on canvas, 1868, Vatican Historical Museum, Lateran Palace. It shows the French and Papal infantry colors (two of the latter) carried by Franco-Papal forces at Mentana in 1867.

32. Illustration from Charette, p. 88 annex, unnumbered color lithograph by F. Appel ("Drapeau du régiment des zouaves pontificaux a Rome"). The book's first edition was printed in Tours and dates from 1875 or 1876. The author has used the second edition, printed in Paris, ca. 1877.

33. Illustration from Vigevano, pl. 1 ("Bandiera del Reggimento Fanteria di linea e del Reggimento Zuavi"); cf. also p. 75. Cf. Ales, p. 89.

34. Illustration from watercolor details in Viviani, plates 7 (Line Infantry) and 9 (Zouaves). Complete illustrations available online (26 July 2018) at: <commons.wikimedia.org/wiki/File:Fanteria_di_linea_pontificia.jpg> and <it.wikipedia.org/wiki/File:Zuavi_pontifici_pre_1870.jpg>. The author's copy of the book does not contain a publisher or date. Those given in the Works Cited come from the listing in the Anne S. K. Brown Military Collection of the Brown University Library in Providence, Rhode Island.

35. Lionel-Noël Royer (1852–1926) befriended Charette and joined the Zouaves after they left papal service and supported France against Prussia in 1871. One of Royer's artistic tableaus with the flag and its guardians appears as a black-and-white frontispiece in Mathuisieulx (1913); with a color version on the cover of Nouaille-Degorce (2017), available online (1 August 2018) at: <editionsedilys.blogspot.com/2016/12/patrick-nouaille-degorce-mentana.html>. His painting, "The Battle Near Mentana" (oil on canvas, ca. 1907, private collection) depicts the flag amid troops, and Charette on horseback. It was exhibited in 1907 in Paris at the *Salon de la Société des Artistes Français*, no. 1396, and was sold by Sotheby's in 2007. Cf. Sotheby's online (retrieved 21 June 2018) at <www.sothebys.com/fr/auctions/ecatalogue/lot.90.html/2007/19th-century-european-paintings-am1030>.

36. Charette, p. 97, reports the ceremonious shredding on 25 September 1870 aboard the frigate l'Orénoque in port at Civitavecchia. Bittard des Portes, p. 241. Rouleau, p. 155. O'Clery, pp. 532–533. Brandani et al, p. 90. Innocenti, p. 43, and email to author, 8 December 2004. Coulombe, pp. 172–173 (shreds preserved).

37. Illustration retrieved online (16 July 2018) at: <www.maquetland.com/article-phototheque/5045-vatican-1861-fanion-bataillon-tirailleur>. The replica is held by the Royal Museum of the Armed Forces and Military History, Brussels, in the display, "Les Belges en Italie, 1860–1870." It also holds a black-and-white photo of the original fanion: "Photo: Drapeau des Tirailleurs Pontificaux Franco-Belges à la Bataille de Castelfidardo le 18 septembre 1860, donné a leur commandant Mr. Le Comte de Becdeliévre par la Sainteté le Pape Pie IX (Italia, 1860)", inventory no. 506279. Cf. also: Defontaine, pp. 35–37 & pl. 4; Brandani et al., pp. 36, 42; Poli, p. 64; Lorenzo Innocenti, email to author, 8 December 2004; Coulombe, p. 100 (who notes that even after Castelfidardo it was blessed by the pope and served the unit for a time).

38. Illustration from Bertrand Malvaux Antiquities, Nantes, Frances, retrieved online (21 June 2018) at: <www.bertrand-malvaux.com/p/20515/banniere-offerte-aux-zouaves-pontificaux-par-une-association-de-femmes-americaines-en-1867-second-empire.html>.

It sold the flag to an unnamed buyer ca. 2015 (reference no. 8733). The flag's inscriptions loosely translate as: "To the Illustrious Army of Zouaves, faithfully safeguarding the Holy See: [given with] the allegiance of the Ladies of America." The medallion in the fly is the *Pro Petri Sede* medal, awarded to veterans of the Battle of Castelfidardo (where the Zouaves' progenitors fought). The flag was made in Rome and was presumably intended to be square until the pole hem was retracted. The flag is recorded in Civiltà Cattolica, anno 18, vol. 11, p. 745f; and anno 19, vol. 2, p. 483f.

39. Illustration from Biteau, p. 16, retrieved online (21 June 2018) at: <lasabretache.fr/wp-content/uploads/2017/08/Les-voluntaires-pontificaux-%C3%A0-cheval.pdf>. The motto beneath Pius' arms is "In hoc signes vinces" (Latin: "Conquer in this sign")—an echo of the legendary sign of the cross at the Battle of Milvian Bridge. The flag's fringe appears to alternate gold and silver sections. It was likely carried at the Battle of Castelfidardo, and was photographed by Gérard Picaud in 1985 in Allier, a French department and the home (in Busset) of Louis Joseph Gaspard de Bourbon-Busset, comte de Chalus (1819–1871), the leader of the "squadron guides" (i.e., "Guides formant l'état-major de l'escadron"). Its current whereabouts is not identified.

40. Ales, p. 88. Brandani et al., p. 30. It was once preserved at the Irish College in Rome.

41. For Dutch Zouave flags, cf. online (retrieved 21 June 2018): "Tilburgse zoeaven ten strijde voor de paus", <www.historietilburg.nl/wp-content/uploads/Jaargang-14-1996-nummer-2.pdf>; and a virtual tour of the Zouaves Museum at Oudenbosch, <zouavenmuseum.nl/museum-documentatie/het-pand/>.

42. Photo, Royal Museum of the Armed Forces and Military History, Brussels, "Drapeau des anciens zouaves pontificaux de la flandre occidentale, Belgique, ca. 1870 [probably ca. 1900, since a motto beneath the arms of Pius IX includes the date 1897]", inventory no. 506440, 135 x 170 cm (53 x 67 in.). Cf. also, "Drapeau de la societé des anciens zouaves pontificaux du pays de Waes", inventory no. 506454.

43. Charette, p. 91. Marraro, pp. 91–93. "Les Zouaves pontificaux du Canada: le drapeau des zouaves canadiens."

44. Musée de la Civilisation, Québec City, inventory no. 1994.8517. It belonged to the "Union Allet"—a veterans' association founded in 1899 and later known as the "Zouaves pontificaux canadiens." Its obverse bears the Zouave badge: a shield with a beaver, maple leaves, and the Zouave motto. Its reverse has yellow-white stripes divided vertically and overlaid by a centered a tiara-and-keys emblem. In all, the museum holds twenty-seven flags and banners preserving the memory of French-Canadian Zouave volunteers. One was created in Montreal in 1868 for Canadian recruits (inventory no. 1994.8507). Its obverse is white with the tiara-and-keys emblem and identifying inscriptions; its reverse bears a beaver and maple leaf emblem. Other flags were produced for Zouave veterans after their return to Canada. Still others replicate the Vatican City flag design, and were perhaps created after 1929 for Zouave descendents and sympathizers. Flag images and collection summary provided by Pauline Grégoire, Documentation Technician, e-mails to author, 22 February 2005 and 28 April 2005.

45. Marius Richard, "La Fedeltà della Francia alla Cattedra di Pietro", 1887, held by the Vatican Historical Museum at the Lateran Palace. The artist signed and dated the painting.

46. The flag is a yellow-white vertical bicolor with the tiara-and-keys emblem centered on the stripes. It bears the inscription *Association des descendants des Zouaves Pontificaux et des Voluntaires de l'Ouest*. See Lucia Flauto, "Zuavi pontifici in visita ai luoghi della Battaglia", *Città di Castelfidardo: sito ufficiale*, 16 April 2010, retrieved online (21 June 2018) at: <www.comune.castelfidardo.an.it/comunicazioni/index.php?id=read&idnews=1805>.

47. Illustration from author's photo. Prince Sforza Ruspoli, e-mail and photos to author, 22 November 2004, and personal interview and photos, Palazzo Ruspoli, Rome, 3 April 2009. A historian suggested the flag is a fort flag in view of its large size. Each vertical breadth is 18" wide. The proportions of the flag (3:4) correspond with those cited for other papal flags and ensigns by LeGras, pl. 22; although *Quadro* appears to suggest 2:3 for the civil ensign (unless annotated thus by the owner of the chart).

48. Ruspoli publicly presented the flag to the Cardinal Secretary of State, Tarcisio Bertone, during festivities for the Vatican Gendarmerie, 29 September 2011, and privately to Benedict XVI the day before. "Vaticano, la bandiera di Porta Pia ritorna dopo 141 anni", La Stampa, 29 September 2011, retrieved online (21 June 2018) at: <www.lastampa.it/2011/09/29/vaticaninsider/ vaticano-la-bandiera-di-porta-pia-ritorna-dopo-anni-hFm3TfE5Jlv1wsrLr7JBhP/pagina.html>. "Il Corpo dell Gendarmeria Vaticana celebra la festa di san Michele Arcangelo", L'Osservatore Romano, 1 October 2011, retrieved online (21 June 2018) at: <www.osservatoreromano. va/it/news/il-corpo-della-gendarmeria-vaticana-celebra-la-fes>. See also, "El comandante de la Gendarmería vaticana: 'No hay amenazas específicas'", video interview by antena3.com with Domenico Giani, Gendarmerie commander, 13 December 2015, retrieved online (21 June 2018) at: <www.antena3.com/noticias/mundo/comandante-gendarmeria-vaticana-hay-amenazas-especificas_2015121300105.html>.

49. Ruspoli learned the flag's history from his grandfather, Prince Alessandro Ruspoli (1869–1952), and surmises that it was lowered at the Villa Paolina and taken to the adjoining Villa Bonaparte. Hoffmann, pp. 419–420, recounts the course of battle at the Villa Paolina, where the white flag was waved by Papal Zouaves after the breach there.

50. Ruspoli inherited the staff with the flag but was unsure whether it was original. It may well have been; indeed, inserting a portable flag-and-staff into a bracket is still a technique used at Vatican sites associated with the Gendarmerie, including its headquarters, barracks, fire station, and courthouse. The wooden staff is about 3 m (10 ft.) long and bears an inlaid pulley at the peak.

51. Dibujo R.Padró, "Roma—Las tropas pontificias piden parlamento por órden de Su Santidad", black-and-white illustration, *La Ilustración Española y Americana*, 5 October 1870 (vol. 14, no. 22), p. 348, retrieved online (21 June 2018) at: <funjdiaz.net/ilustracion/?pag=37>; and in color, Getty Images no. 513680703, retrieved online (21 June 2018) at: <www.gettyimages.com/detail/ news-photo/italian-unification-pontifical-troops-ask-parliament-by-news-photo/513680703>.

52. "Siége et capitulation de Cività-Castellana", p. 598, where the flag was described by an Italian soldier and eyewitness on 13 September, the day following its surrender. Beauffort, p. 179, reports that Papal Zouaves shredded the fort's "white and yellow flag" to prevent its capture, and distributed the pieces as relics—as they likewise did with their infantry color after the fall of Rome.

53. "ITALY, the Papal Authority Proclaimed", New York *Daily Tribune*, 10 August 1849, p. 2. In Rome the flags were raised to cannon salutes at the Campidoglio tower (where the Republican assembly met) and the Castel Sant'Angelo fortress, on 15 July at 3:30 p.m.: cf. *Giornale di Roma*, 14 July (p. 29), 16 July (p. 33f), and 17 July (p. 38); *Raccolta delle leggi … dello Stato Romano*, p. 114; Ghisi, p. 239f. The flag design may also be reflected in a medal presented to foreign troops who aided the Papal States restoration in 1849. It consisted of a bicolor ribbon attached to a medallion with the tiara-and-keys emblem on one side; cf. online (retrieved 21 June 2018) at: <www.mymilitaria.it/ liste_03/1850_medaglia_pio_IX.htm>.

54. Martina, p. 378f, records that in mid-July papal authorities had insisted on the flags to clarify French intentions to restore papal sovereignty, since only French flags were flying in Rome immediately after the occupation. Kertzer, *The Pope who would be King*, records different approaches to the papal flag, taken by the foreign armies of the restoration: pp. 180, 200, 205, 211, 228, 238, 249, 256, 261, 405 (n. 4), 409 (n.15).

55. "The Pope and His Probable Future", which reports the handover date as 10 December; but the flag ceremony took place on 11 December at 8:00 a.m. according to *The Times* of London (cf. "Departure of the French Troops from Rome"), and *Civiltà Cattolica*, anno 18, vol. 9, pp. 104 & 123 (which records that the French flag was taken down from the main "door" where a guardhouse stood, while the papal flag was hoisted atop the fort on the mast by the archangel's statue). Cf. Gregorovius, p. 268; and "The French Leave the Castle of St. Angelo". In October 1867 French forces returned to help papal forces repel Garibaldi's, and both French and Papal flags are reported atop the fortress; cf. Gregorovius, p. 302, and Bittard des Portes, p. 138.

56. Illustration detail from "Les troupes françaises évacuent le fort Saint-Ange, le 11 décembre. D'après un croquis de M. Zwahlen", black-and-white engraving in *L'Illustration: Le Journal Universal*, vol. 48, no. 1244 (29 December 1866), p. 404; see also p. 402. Image retrieved online (21 June 2018) at: <repository.library.brown.edu/studio/item/bdr:214524/>. The fort clock reads 8:00—the exact morning hour of the flag ceremony.

57. Illustration from author's photo, 2009. Cf. Vatican Historical Museum inventory no. 30615. A linen fragment from a flag taken from the tower (torre) of the same fort may correspond with missing fragments from the one preserved by the Vatican. It is preserved by the Museo Civio del Risorgimento in Modena (catalog no. 811, measuring 15.5 x 20 cm [6 x 8 in.]).

58. "Italy and the Papacy", pp. 82 & 93, reports the fort's surrender on the afternoon of 21 September, when the flag was lowered. This is reflected in the date on the Museum placard too. Kertzer, *Prisoner of the Vatican*, pp. 38–49, 59–62, explains the delayed surrender: Italy initially desired the pope to retain sovereignty over the Leonine City, including the fortress. The bersagliere is recorded by the Museo Nazionale di Castel Sant'Angelo on Facebook, retrieved online (21 June 2018) at <www.facebook.com/419533098197881/photos/a.422262721258252.1073741829.419533098197881/559804544170735/>.

59. Corona reports that the flag was preserved by Baron Wilhelm Christian Wedel-Jarlsberg (1852–1909), a Norwegian nobleman who converted to Catholicism, became a papal chamberlain in 1882, and lived in Rome. He gave it to his daughter Carmen (1885–1957) who married Senator Antonio Boggiano Pico (1873–1965). Their family donated it to Pope John Paul II during his visit to Genoa on 22 September 1985.

60. *Giornale militare officiale*, pp. 839–845, lists fortress protocols from 1866 with directives for "papal flag" use, including occasions for display and cannon salute protocols; but there are no descriptions of the flag's design or legal origin. Cf. Vigevano, pp. 807–813.

61. Generic references to the papal flag (with no design details) exist in accounts of unrest nationwide. Rome: Chigi, 26 November 1848 entry, reported that the "papal flag" was hoisted at Castel Sant'Angelo "as usual for the feast day" (Sunday)—one day after Pius IX had departed for exile in Gaeta. Ravenna and Ferrara: Cesare, pp. 235–236, reports that in 1859 the "papal flag" was lowered in major forts and piazzas.

62. Another variant perhaps bisected the stripes with the arms of Pius IX, akin to similar civil flags and military colors: *Civiltà Cattolica*, anno 12, vol. 11, p. 742, reports similar civil flags during a papal visit to Piazza del Popolo on 8 September 1861; and for military

colors, see Figs. 2.12, 2.19–20, & 2.33–35. A vessel carrying the pontiff in 1842 wears a vertical bicolor bisected by his arms in an anonymous 1842 painting held by the Museo di Roma, "5 settembre 1842, Gregorio XVI visita i primi tre vapori inglesi arrivati al porto di Ripa grande," retrieved online (21 June 2018) at <https://commons.wikimedia.org/wiki/File:Pal_Braschi_-_Ripa_Grande_Gregorio_XVI_e_i_primi_3_vapori_inglesi_(ignoto,_1842)_P1090712.JPG>. Perhaps papal Ancona also had its own papal fort flag—see p. 25—although a makeshift yellow-white flag of unspecified design was posted from a lighthouse turret during the Battle of Ancona in 1860 (Quatrebarbes, p. 230f; Alvarez, p. 134f).

63. LeGras, pl. 22, nos. 3 & 8.

64. *Don Pirlone a Roma* (a polemic on the Roman Revolution) carries satirical sketches that consistently identify the papal fort flag as white with Pius' pontifical arms: cf. Pinto, vol. 2, pl. 170 (Bologna); and vol. 3, pl. 201 (Rome, Porta San Pancrazio); pl. 206 (Rome, Castel Sant'Angelo—but not the fort flag; rather a vexillum for the bastion); pl. 273 (Civitavecchia). An eyewitness to Roman unrest in the summer of 1848 reported that "the white banner of the Pope" flew from the Capitoline Hill's Campidoglio tower—but beneath a larger Italian tricolor that was "held high above the white banner" by the tower's statue (MacFarlane, p. 5).

65. See "View of the political confinement of Civita Castellana fort, on the evening of June 21, 1846, the day of Pope Pius IX's coronation", watercolor print, 19th century, Bologna, Museo Civico del Risorgimento, retrieved online (21 June 2018) at <www.gettyimages.com/detail/news-photo/view-of-the-political-confinement-of-civita-castellana-fort-news-photo/534983201>. The original Italian title is, "'I detunuti politici nel forte di Civita Castellana, all'annunzio dell'amnistia accordata da Pio IX, preparano la sera del 21 luglio 1846 festosa illuminazione' (Litografia del tempo nel Museo del Risorgimento, Bologna)", as in *L'Italia nei cento anni*, p. 1224.

66. Willes, on 21 July 1849: "The Papal flag (white) was rehoisted here [Civitavecchia] under a salute of 100 guns on the 15th [of July] …. I have visited Rome …. The Papal flag (white and yellow) was rehoisted on the 15th, and is still flying on the Capitol Quirinal [sic], but the French flag predominates in Rome as far as numbers are concerned." Bicolors at both the Campidoglio and the Castel Sant'Angelo are also reported by *Gazzetta di Mantova*, p. 239, and *L'Araldo*. See also the similar report from the New York *Daily Tribune*, 10 August 1849, p. 2, as above.

67. *Revue Catholique de l'Alsace: Année 1862*, p. 290: Abbot Joseph Guerber reported a "yellow and white" flag alongside that of France at the "old bastions" of the fort.

68. Innocenti, p. 44, includes a watercolor signed and dated (29 April 1862) by a Papal Zouave composer. A Zouave encampment is near the fort, which flies a bicolor with white at the hoist (reported correctly?).

69. "Siége et Capitulation de Cività-Castellana", p. 598, as detailed above.

70. In 1868, Canadian Zouave recruits were told to change their native unit color, from white to yellow-and-white (see p. 51). Were white flags considered obsolete on land? Or did their flag compete with that of the Noble Guard (which also had a white field)?

71. Appendices I & II show consistently vertical bicolors after the Papal States restoration in 1849; including flags of the infantry, Palatine Guard, forts, merchant ships, and state vessels; cf. also Fig. 2.42.

72. See p.52, concerning Canadian Zouaves, French Zouave descendants, and the painting by Marius Richard.

73. See pp. 90–93. In 1929 Italian flagmakers were familiar with both vertical and horizontal yellow-white bicolors, whose stripes were overlaid by a centered tiara-and-keys emblem (see p. 95).

74. Both appeared in a display titled "Roma 1846–1849" held in Rome in 1987 and commemorated in *Roma 1846–1849*, pp. 23, 39. Illustration from A. Viviani (?)", Pio IX si reca alla cappella papale di Santa Maria del Popolo" ("Pius IX is borne to the papal chapel of Santa Maria del Popolo"), undated painting of an 8 September 1846 event, Museo di Roma, no. 4202: portrays Pius' cortege leading him through the Piazza del Popolo, underneath an arch erected in his honor; the surrounding buildings are bedecked in yellow-white vertical bicolors and members of the crowd carry them as well. (A comparable scene is described in *Il mondo illustrato*, 16 January 1847, p. 40, where bicolors bear the inscription *Viva Pio IX*) A. Malchiodi, "Ciceruacchio [symbolic figure of the people] announces to the people that Pius IX has conceded the [Fundamental] Statute [i.e., constitution]", oil-painting dating from 1877, Museo di Roma, no. 131, portrays an event of 14 March 1848, viz. the announcement of the constitution in the same piazza, with similar yellow-white flags (some horizontal) alongside Italian tricolors.

75. "Drapeaux pontificaux", p. 99 (published in 1909), calls them "merchant flags"— apparently meaning not the civil or state ensigns proper, but yellow-white flags in collective contradistinction to flags "of the pope himself which were white". Cf. contemporary accounts by Gregorovius, pp. 135 (1861), 150 (1861), 152 (1862), 325 (1869).

76. Cf. Il 1*2 Aprile 1867 a Roma*, esp. pp. 31–32 and a lithograph of a naval salute at Rome's Porto di Ripeta, where a pavilion is decked out in vertical yellow-white bicolors (between pp. 26 & 27). Vertical bicolors may have predominated where French forces protected papal rule under their vertical tricolor; and horizontal bicolors may have flourished in northern regions where Austrian forces provided protection under their horizontally-striped flag (the Hapsburg civil flag was black over yellow). It may be worth noting that Hanover flew a bicolor of yellow over white.

77. Museum catalog no. 795, cotton fabric, ca. 1840/1850, available online (27 June 2018) at: <bbcc.ibc.regione.emilia-romagna.it/pater/loadcard.do?id_card=67606>. Early in the reign of Pius IX, a similar flag represented a district of Siena in connection with the Palio competition: cf. "I costumi", *Contrada della Tartuca*, retrieved online (5 August 2010) at: <www.tartuca.it/joomla/contrada/storia> and available via <archive.org>.

78. *Del danno che avverrebbe allo Stato Pontificio*, frontpiece.

79. Illustration from *Verzameling*, n. 18 ("Romeinsche Signaal-vlag om communicatie met de wal te er langen"). In 1843 Flaggen-Almanack, pl. 15, identified a plain yellow flag as the Papal States "private" flag. Did it intend a plain yellow-white bicolor? Does "private" imply a civil flag? In 1843 Massimo, p. 42, reports two yellow-white flags during a tour of Gregory XVI to Zagarolo in Lazio.

80. Below, Chapter 3.

81. For example, the British Union Flag originated for use at sea. Use on land was first authorized for forts in 1800 (probably confirming existing practice), and only sometime later migrated to state buildings—which was only codified in 1902, amid some uncertainty about flag use ashore. See online (retrieved 21 June 2018) at "Flags of the World", at <www.crwflags.com/fotw/flags/gb-use.html>.

82. Cf. Pinto, vol. 2, pl. 170 (Bologna).

83. Illustration from, "La bandera pontificia en Buenos Aires", retrieved online (3 July 2000) at: <hemerotecadigital.bne.es/issue.vm?id=0004099857&page=22&search=bandera+pa

pal&lang=es>. The flag pictured is in the Argentine proportions (ca. 1:2) and attached to a movable staff. Cardinale, p. 284f, notes that Papal States consuls held naval ranks; might they thus have employed the war ensign or naval jack if a flag was needed?

84. See pp. 90–91, 93.

85. Illustration from Piroli, ms. 72/22 (1829); reproduced with permission (Istituto per la Storia del Risorgimento Italiano). Vigevano, p. 73. Ales, pp. 86–87, 386–387 (pl. 108), states they received a flag "immediately" after being reconstituted under Pius VII on 17 December 1815, but *Fedeltà Palatina* specifies 1818. Appendix II herein presumes the same flag was used under Leo XII in 1823 (as shown by Piroli), but with his new arms (often painted over the previous pope's); see Piroli, ms. 72/2 (1823), retrieved online (30 June 2018) at: <www.internetculturale.it/it/16/search/detail?instance=magindice &case=&id=oai%3Awww.internetculturale.sbn.it%2FTeca%3A20%3ANT0000%3 ARM0135_DIG_2774&qt>.

86. Illustration from Piroli, ms. 72/33 (1831), reproduced with permission (Istituto per la Storia del Risorgimento Italiano). Cf. also ms. 72/37 (1832). *Pace* Vigevano, p. 73 (who mistakes the color of the fringe and stars). *Pace* Ales, pp. 87 & 386–387, pl. 108 (who mistakes the flag's design: it was divided from upper fly to lower hoist, not vice versa; and its obverse and reverse did not differ in design).

87. Piroli, ms. 72/60 (1841).

88. Illustration from author's photos, 2009 (the flag's obverse and reverse sides are indicated differently in the museum inventory, versus the flag as displayed in a double-sided display frame, and as photographed for the museum archive). Cf. *Il mondo illustrato*, 16 January 1847, pp. 34, 48; and 31 July 1847, p. 484. *L'Italia nei cento anni*, vol. 45, p. 1266.

89. The white cravat is edged with golden branches. At the bottom, one side bears a rampant lion (as in Bologna's provincial arms) holding a yellow and red vexillum beneath the inscription I BOLOGNESI; while the other bears the Capitoline wolf beneath the inscription AI ROMANI.

90. Illustration from author's photo. *Roma 1846–1849*, pp. 14, 35–38, including a photo of an 1847 labarum in the Capitoline Museum collections (fig. 52). Piroli, ms. 76/24. Vigevano, p. 74. Zara, p. 136. The flags are displayed in the Palazzo Senatorio, Sala del Sindaco (known as the "Sala delle Bandiere"), retrieved online (21 June 2018) at: <www. museicapitolini.net/records_collocation.xql?structure=Palazzo+Senatorio&substructure =Sala+delle+Bandiere>.

91. Illustration from "Figurini, uniformi ed emblemi della Guardia Civica Romana", Istituto per la Storia del Risorgimento Italiano, Museo Centrale del Risorgimento di Roma, Sezione Iconografica, Cassetta II (49–51 at 50); reproduced with permission. See also, "Figurini, uniformi ed emblemi della Guardia Civica Romana", online (retrieved 16 June 2018) at: <www.risorgimento.it//shades/htm/dettaglioCartellaRic.php?idCARTELLA=188164> and <www.risorgimento.it//shades/htm/dettaglioCartellaRic.php?idCARTELLA=188163>. *Roma 1846–1849*, pp. 14, 36–38. Vigevano, p. 75. *Gazzetta di Roma*, 20 March 1848, p. 1. Ghisi, p. 232. The Museo del Risorgimento of Forlí also holds a local Civic Guard labarum with a tricolor cravat, as exhibited online (retrieved 29 August 2018) at: <http:// bbcc.ibc.regione.emilia-romagna.it/pater/loadcard.do?id_card=125860>. Secondary sources (Ghisi, pl. 17; Colangeli, fig. 18) mistakenly show the labarum with the Italian colors on the reverse—which is unconfirmed by primary sources except when the papal arms were replaced by the Roman wolf during the Roman Republic (e.g., Piroli, ms. 76/70).

92. Piroli, 76/32 [Frascati, 1848]. Cf. Crociani, pp. 419, 424.

93. Illustration from postcard of work of Faustino Joli, "Sottotenente alfiere della Legione Bolognese (1848–1849)", ca. 1849, oil on canvas, Museo Civico del Risorgimento, Bologna. Cf. Piroli, ms. 76/28 [Bologna, 1848, same design].

94. Illustration from "bandiera", Battaglione Universitario di Bologna, silk fragment, Museo Civico del Risorgimento di Bologna, no. 2537, retrieved online (27 June 2018) at: <bbcc. ibc.regione.emilia-romagna.it/pater/loadcard.do?id_card=177446>. That pictured is one fragment; a second one bears an inscription with the battalion's name, and the date 1848, framed by a laurel wreath; presumably one is from the obverse and the other is from the reverse. Cf. *Catalogo degli oggetti*, p. 98.

95. Illustration from author's photo, 1993. Piroli, ms. 77/22. *Regolamento della Guardia Palatina* carries the Holy See's authorization on 7 September (p. 22), and the Guard's daily orders repeated it on 12 September (p. 32); but neither reports design details. *Civiltà Cattolica* anno 11, vol.6 (1860), p. 223, reports a procession with the flag in Rome on the day after its blessing. Usai, pp. 167–169. *Fedeltà palatina*. Ales, pp. 89–90, 390–391 (pl. 110). *Guide to the Vatican Museums*, pp. 155–156. Governatorato, pp. 203, 403.

96. See "Restoration Projects", p. 1; also, "The Palatine Flag", *Patrons of the Arts in the Vatican Museums* (website), 12 October 2015, retrieved online (21 June 2018) at: www.vatican-patrons. org/the-palatine-flag-3831>. See preliminary restored version via the Patrons of the Arts in the Vatican Museums on Facebook, retrieved online (21 June 2018) at: <www.facebook. com/131874896849296/photos/a.131891543514298.11029.131874896849296/881890581 847720/?type=3>.

97. Author's photo of Palatine Guard colors from the pontificates of Pius IX to Paul VI. "Lettera del Santo Padre Paolo VI al Cardinale Giovanni Villot per il servizio d'ordine e di vigilanza nella Città del Vaticano", 14 September 1970, retrieved online (21 June 2018) at <www.vatican.va/ holy_father/paul_vi/letters/1970/documents/hf_p-vi_let_19700914_vigilanza-vaticano_it.html>.

98. Illustration from author's photo, 1987. The flags are displayed in the Palazzo Senatorio, Sala del Sindaco (known as the "Sala delle Bandiere"), retrieved online (21 June 2018) at: <www.museicapitolini.net/records_collocation.xql?structure=Palazzo+Senatorio& substructure=Sala+delle+Bandiere>.

99. Quoted in *Roma 1846–1849*, p. 34. The district names as they appear on the flags photographed by the author are Monti, Trevi, Colonna, Campo Marzio, Ponte, Parione, Regola, S. Eustachio, Pigna, Campitelli, S. Angelo, Ripa, Trastevere, and Borgo. Additional flags for Ponte Ricola and Lampitelli included their names on a silverish-blue medallion.

100. Pius IX, motu proprio, 2 October 1848, art. 40, quoted in *Roma 1846–1849*, p. 34. The decree also specifies that the district flags "will be displayed as usual on the occurrences and carried … by the fourteen chosen among the most upright inhabitants as named by the magistrature" and to "accompany the solemn procession of the octave of the Most Holy Body of the Lord at the church of St. Mark, and in other circumstances" (Art. 28). For anecdotal mention, cf. Chigi, 17 June 1847 entry, etc.

101. Illustration from author's photo, 1993. Vigevano, p. 76 and plate 2, notes that it was vertically disposed, although displayed from an upright staff. Likewise Brandani et al, pp. 90 & 92. Piroli, ms. 79/72 (1853), and Ales, 90, 396–397 (pl. 113), show its design disposed upright instead of vertically. Zara, p. 137. *Guide to the Vatican Museums*, p. 156.

102. Illustration from author's photo, 1993, of the flag retired in 1870. Vigevano, p. 76 and pl. 3, states that it was vertically disposed, although displayed from an upright staff. Zara, p. 137. Brandani et al, pp. 90 & 92. *Guide to the Vatican Museums*, p. 156. Wise, no. 333 and p.

152 (where he suggests it dates from about 1865). Ales, p. 90 (states that it dates from the 1860s), 396–397 (pl. 113).

103. Illustration from Francisco Gregoric, used with permission. Ales, pp. 396–397 (pl. 113, with the arms of Pius VIII); cf. p. 90 which states that it was 60 cm (24 in.) square. However Piroli, ms. 79/30 (1826, with the arms of Leo XII), shows a small oblong flag. Wise, no. 332 and p. 152. Governatorato, p. 214.

104. Inventory no. 54713, ca. 90 x 90 cm (35 x 35 in.). Author's photo, 1993. The earliest reference to the flag known to the author appears in 1909 in "Drapeaux pontificaux", p. 98, note 1. Lancellotti, *Mondo Vaticano*, p. 138, provides information on the original and the copy. *Guide to the Vatican Museums*, p. 156. Governatorato, p. 214. Alvarez, pp. 72–74.

105. Illustration from Francisco Gregoric, used with permission. Lancellotti, *La corte pontificia*, p. 155, shows the standard under Pius XI, as followed here; the trophy pattern seems to vary in flags afterward, as does the direction of the cravat's inscription. Ales, pp. 388–389 (pl. 109); cf. p. 91. Piroli, ms. 71/17 (1837). "Drapeaux pontificaux", p. 98. *Guide to the Vatican Museums*, pp. 155–156. Museum photos. Governatorato, p. 200. Chigi, 2 April 1848 entry, says the flag bore a cravat in the Italian colors during the events of that period.

106. No. 29457. *Guide to the Vatican Museums*, p. 156.

107. Illustration from Piroli, ms. 71/8 (1831, Gregory XVI); cf. also ms. 76/3 (1847, Pius IX). Galbreath, p. 60. "Drapeaux pontificaux", p. 100, states that Pius VII introduced the stars, but this is not verified by the actual standard preserved from his pontificate.

108. *Verzameling*, no. 7 (1834 illustration from a 1705 Amsterdam chart). Cf. L'Art de Batir (1719), pl. 62; *A Display of the Naval Flags*, pl. 6; *Flaggen-Almanack*, pl. 15.

109. Gabriele Cardinal Ferretti, Secretary of State, "Summary of the Honorific Preogatives of the Roman Senate", 3 October 1847, art. 28, 30, in *Atti del Sommo Pontifice*.

110. Gasbarri, p. 198.

111. Rangoni-Machiavelli, p. 77. Charts attesting this flag are pre-1800: c.f. *Banderas; A Display of the Naval Flags*, pl. 6.

112. "Italy and the Papacy", p. 80, reports that white flags were hoisted from the "cross at the apex of the lantern of S. Peter's [Basilica] … and also on the battlements of S. Angelo, and the lofty campanile of S. Maria Maggiore", and carried by a "mounted officer to the Porta Pia" (cf. p. 91); pp. 82 & 93 reports that the fortress surrendered on the afternoon of 21 September 1870 (when the papal flag was lowered), while the white flag flew until Italy's was raised on 29 September. Cf. Innocenti, pp. 118, 122–123.

113. See illustration, "1863—Bandiere per le fortezze, torri e stabilimenti militari", *Ministero della Difesa—Republica Italiana*, online (21 June 2018) at: <www.difesa.it/Area_Storica_HTML/UniformiTradizioni/Pagine/1863BandiereFortezzeTorriMilitari.aspx>.

Figure 3.1. Proto-National Papal Flag, postcard, early 1900s

Figure 3.2. Proto-National Papal Flag, the Vatican, Cortile di San Damaso, Pius X, 1903 (photo & detail)

Chapter 3
Vatican City (1870–Today)

The Roman Question

 After Italian forces captured Rome on 20 September 1870, the pope surrendered all his armed forces (except his household guards), but not his claim to sovereignty or land. Popes had governed the Eternal City since the Roman Empire had ended, and its unprovoked seizure—despite Italian promises not to do so—was galling. Rome now became the capital of an Italian king who took over the pope's Quirinal Palace, while anti-clericalists held state offices flying the tricolor flag promoting the House of Savoy.

The challenge of whether pope or king should rule the city was called the "Roman Question" among vying European powers well before 1870. Afterward they jockeyed to support either Italy, whose unity was fragile, or the Holy See, which distrusted Italy's ascendancy. The popes viewed their sovereignty as a guarantee of right religion, Rome as Catholicism's spiritual capital, and themselves as guardians of the martyrs' tombs.

Indeed, the era's popes insisted on the return of *all* papal lands seized during Italy's *Risorgimento*. In hindsight that goal seems unrealistic, but at the time it was less clearly so. Three times within a century, popes had lost their state to French or Roman revolutionaries (1796, 1808, and 1848); and each time had recovered it. Since shifting geopolitics had repeatedly vindicated papal claims in the past, why think otherwise now? Hence popes often appealed to foreign powers for the return of the Papal States.[1]

By contrast, Italy maintained that Romans preferred Italian rule and held a plebiscite to confirm that claim. The Kingdom initially proposed substantial papal jurisdiction over the "Leonine City"—an area within the two Leonine walls that form a conduit between the Vatican and the Tiber River. Its final position was less generous, as codified in parliament's "Law of Guarantees"

(1871). Henceforth the pope's person was deemed inviolable—but not his property. Papal holdings at the Vatican and elsewhere were to be treated with discretion by Italian authorities, and were deemed inviolable—but not sovereign.

Precedent for such discretion was at hand. When Italian General Nino Bixio captured the Papal States port of Civitavecchia on 15 September 1870, he ordered that the papal warship *Immacolata Concezione* remain inviolate as a papal yacht should the pope opt for foreign exile. But he also ordered that it "change its flag from that of the state to the personal [flag] of the Pope."[2] The flags in question are uncertain,[3] since only its war ensign and jack are preserved.[4]

The popes, however, rejected Italian assurances about their personal inviolability as a unilateral concession that could be revoked at will. After all, the king had promised not to seize Rome in the first place, and the Law of Guarantees avoided real questions of sovereign and extraterritorial rights. In protest, the popes cloistered themselves behind the Vatican walls for nearly sixty years, never appearing in public even in St. Peter's Square (with rare exception). For Catholics worldwide, their absence was painful and required a solution.

The matter was finally resolved in 1929 when the Lateran Accords reconciled the Holy See and Italy, established Vatican City State, and regularized Italian Catholicism. The pontifs of this era included Pius IX, Leo XIII, Pius X, Benedict XV, and Pius XI; their reigns are listed in Appendix VII.

Papal Flags: 1870–1929

During the Roman Question period (1870–1929), several papal flags remained in use at the Vatican. Early references often lack details, or reflect the Swiss Guard flag;[5] but never the design eventually adopted by Vatican City. Instead, from at least 1903, such references denote a proto-national papal flag,[6] a yellow-white vertical bicolor overlaid by a centered tiara-and-keys emblem, as in a contemporary Swiss postcard (Fig. 3.1).[7]

Use of this flag reinforced the Holy See's claims to sovereignty, absent territory.[8] It flew over some Papal States forts until 1870 and was considered for adoption by Vatican City in 1929, but was set aside and replaced.[9] (For a time it appeared even after 1929—sometimes in square format, like the new Vatican City flag.[10]) It is pictured at the Argentine papal legation in 1900 (see

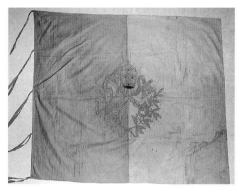

Figure 3.3. Proto-National Papal Flag, after 1900, detail at right

Figure 3.4 (sides). Proto-National Papal Flag, Italian, undated
Figure 3.5 (center). Proto-National Papal Flag, Brescia, undated

Fig. 2.27)[11] and in the Apostolic Palace courtyard, Cortile di San Damaso—apparently first under Pius X (Fig. 3.2).[12] There it appears at papal audiences from 1903 to 1929,[13] as well as other events.[14]

Private collections, such as the Zaricor Flag Collection, hold several specimens of this flag (Fig. 3.3).[15] Though labeled "Pontifical States military color" by a consultant, its provenance is unclear. Its emblem is appliquéd in yellow within a wreath—and only on the obverse of the flag; five yellow ties are attached to the hoist. A museum acquired it in 1912, with no further information about its origins.

Two further specimens are held by the author. Both have ties at the hoist with embroidered tiara-and-keys emblems, and both are nearly square (and thus may date from after 1929). The first is a wool flag with sewn stripes. It belonged to a cardinal who served in Rome, but his name and tenure are uncertain (Fig. 3.4).[16] A larger prototype is shown in an undated photo of Collegio

Figure 3.6. Proto-National Papal Flag, Italian, undated

Figure 3.7. Proto-National Papal Flag, Vatican dinner, undated

Cesare Arici in Brescia, a Catholic school attended by Paul VI in his boyhood (Fig. 3.5).[17] The second specimen is a silk flag with printed stripes (Fig. 3.6).[18] The author also holds an undated photo of the proto-national flag above a bust of Pius XI at a Vatican dinner that included Palatine Guards (Fig. 3.7).[19]

Some flag sources from the Roman Question period report the use of a plain bicolor, presumably as a civil flag in the Vatican area, and supposedly disposed horizontally white over yellow.[20] This corresponds to plain bicolors (vertical or horizontal) used as civil flags in the Papal States. An illustrated postcard from 1925 shows such bicolors flying in the Vatican's Cortile della Pigna. They hang vertically from crossbars, with stripes running lengthwise, and swallowtails at the bottom.[21]

Papal militia colors during the Roman Question period included those of the Palatine Honor Guard Corps, the Noble Guard Corps and the Pontifical Gendarme Corps. Each flag has been described previously.[22] They were altered with each new pope until September 1970, when they fell into disuse after Paul VI disbanded the first two groups (although the police service was maintained). The Swiss Guard retained its distinctive flags, as described below, along with a recent, new gendarmerie flag. A Standard of the Holy Roman Church appears as late as 1958—a red, swallow-tailed banner bearing the umbrella-and-keys device in gold, amid golden six-pointed stars (see Fig. 9.1).[23] Until 1963, the Marshal of the Holy Roman Church displayed a white flag with his coat of arms at papal conclaves, as their guardian.[24]

Beyond the Vatican, some papal diplomats flew papal flags—perhaps the proto-national design, as in Argentina, where it was lowered when diplomatic relations ruptured (1885) and re-hoisted when they resumed (1900, see Fig. 2.27).[25] Ships carrying church dignitaries flew unspecified papal flags at times.[26] Catholics worldwide flew them too. In Modena a handheld papal flag (ca. 1920) was white (at the hoist) and yellow (at the fly).[27] In France unspecified yellow-white flags flew upon Joan of Arc's beatification (1909), resulting in arrests for using flags of an unrecognized sovereign (relations between France and the Vatican having ended).[28] U.S. flagmakers offered various yellow-white papal flags for sale during this period—such as the former civil ensign, or a vertical bicolor with the pope's personal arms centered on the stripes[29] or on the white stripe.[30] A fringed flag of the latter design with the arms of Pius XI, is held by the Vatican.[31] Some Italian flagmakers also sold papal flags.

*Figure 3.8 Plain Vertical Bicolor,
12 February 1929, Rome*

*Figure 3.9 Plain Horizontal
Bicolor, 11 February 1929, Milan*

*Figure 3.10. Artistic Template for Vatican flag drafts, 1929 (Vigevano's illustration
of final Papal States Infantry Color)*

Selecting a Vatican Flag

In 1929 the Lateran Treaty resolved the Roman Question: the Holy See recognized Italy, and obtained sovereignty over "Vatican City State" (*lo Stato della Città del Vaticano*)—along with extraterritorial jurisdiction over several properties in or near Rome, including key papal offices, shrines, and educational institutions. Signed on 11 February at the Lateran Palace, the treaty surprised a delighted public, and awaited certain ratification in June. To celebrate the historic *conciliazione*, papal flags and banners briefly appeared alongside Italy's at Roman public buildings. A photo from 12 February shows a plain vertical bicolor flying alongside Italy's state flag (with the royal arms) at Palazzo Chigi, the contemporary seat of its foreign ministry in Rome (Fig. 3.8).[32] However, in a similar display at Milan's Central Post Office, the papal bicolor was divided horizontally instead (Fig. 3.9).[33]

Soon, Vatican authorities were queried about the "correct" papal flag by diplomats, flagmakers, and Italian officials. Deliberations were managed by the papal secretariat of state, as attested by a Vatican Secret Archives dossier.[34] Some queried the precise flag design, especially whether (and where) the tiara-and-keys emblem appeared. Indeed, Italian flagmakers were familiar with the proto-national papal flag attested earlier, as well as a variant divided horizontally.[35] A few asked whether the pope had a personal flag distinct from a flag of state; but most presumed that "the" papal flag was a single, uniform design.

Initially, papal authorities seemed unsure, despite the proto-national papal flag flying at the apostolic palace. Instead the Roman Curia coordinator (*Sostituto*) first replied that "the" papal flag was a plain vertical bicolor with a special staff and cravat.[36] His description precisely reflected a flag sketch in a recent book on the Papal States army by Attilio Vigevano (the final papal infantry color, Fig. 3.10).[37] But on 24 February, a brief study of papal flags (note the plural) by Pio Pagliucchi instead recommended that Vatican City adopt the ensign flown by Papal States merchant ships until 1870—a yellow-white vertical bicolor with the tiara-and-keys emblem on the white stripe.[38]

A historian, Pagliucchi clearly enjoyed the favor of the authorities. In a twist of fate, his father had commanded the papal fort at Castel Sant'Angelo in 1870 as a papal flag was lowered for the last time.[39] Pagliucchi's recommendation was apparently accepted, since by 11 March the cardinal secretary himself circulated a draft papal flag design to other pontifical authorities. This likely

Figure 3.11. Vatican flag design drafts, 1929.
From left to right: "Bandiera militare", "Bandiera dello Stato", "Non esatta"

followed his review of three sketches based on Pagliucchi's study (Fig. 3.11).[40] Each imitated Vigevano's artistic template: a square vertical bicolor with a yellow staff bearing a lance-head and a yellow-white cravat. Artistic flourishes were added to the original staff (golden spiral braid) and finial (an angel's head). The Vatican City constitutional illustration retained this flag format.

One draft version was a plain bicolor inscribed "military flag" (*Bandiera militare*)—which had served as the final Papal States infantry color. The second draft overlaid the bicolor with a centered tiara-and-keys emblem—i.e., the proto-national papal flag, a Papal States fort flag that the Vatican had revived. Lacking attestation in Pagliucchi's study, it was inscribed "inexact" (*Non esatta*)—as opposed to a bicolor with the emblem on the white stripe that comprised the third draft. It was inscribed "flag of the state" (*Bandiera dello Stato*)—doubtless due to his recommendation.

(A draft of the pope's "personal" flag went no further, likely because the Noble Guard color was similar. It was a square white color bearing his personal arms and golden flourishes along the edges, with a suitable staff and cravat.[41])

Pagliucchi's logic was flawed but defensible. Seeking a precedent for a flag "of the State"—perhaps as distinct from a personal standard—he relied heavily on an 1855 decree stipulating that merchant marine vessels flying an award flag at the masthead, should fly that "of the State" (*dello Stato [Pontificio]*) at the stern—meaning the civil ensign of 1825.[42] He thus concluded that "this and none other" was the flag "of the [Papal] State".

Here he erred. No particular, exclusive flag "of the State" existed in the 1800s; and there was little distinction between a "personal" or "national" papal flag in the Papal States. Instead the term *bandiera pontificia* referred generically to many flags "of the State", despite varying designs—whether for merchant ships, coast guard vessels, warships, forts, infantry units, or other militias (see Appendices I & II). Indeed throughout history, a "papal flag" conveyed a symbolic concept (i.e., papal sovereignty) more than a specific or uniform design—despite shared design elements; all were arguably flags of the state.

Reviving a civil ensign was likewise anomalous, since it would henceforth fly mainly at papal offices—a custom rarely seen before 1903.[43] Yet even for a landlocked Vatican state, a former maritime ensign was a reasonable flag. It once flew widely from ships that conveyed papal statehood,[44] its colors were pontifical, and its emblem was unvarying—unlike a pontiff's personal arms that changed with each pontificate. While this precise design never flew ashore in the 1800s, other yellow-white flags did—including military colors from the time of Gregory XVI and fort flags under Pius IX. Collectively and despite various designs, yellow-white flags had clearly come to symbolize modern papal sovereignty.[45]

Henceforth, however, the term "papal flag" would denote a uniform, unvarying design—a first for the modern era—a design also commonly called "the Vatican flag" (a descriptor previously unknown).

The Vatican Flag Design

On 7 June 1929 the Lateran Treaty took effect upon the solemn exchange of ratification records. The same day, the Vatican City constitution (*Legge Fondamentale*) was signed by Pius XI and was entered into the Holy See's official gazette.[46] It revived the former Papal States civil ensign as the new Vatican flag, as counseled by Pagliucchi's study. Apparently the flag did not fly immediately, probably because it had to be produced, and buildings fitted with flagstaffs; but a month later it is recorded at the new papal embassy to Italy.[47]

Figure 3.12. Constitution, 1929, Annex A

Figure 3.13. Constitution, 2000, Annex A

The flag was reconfirmed in a revised constitution issued in 2000.[48] Identical to the 1929 version, the article pertaining to the flag reads:

> The Vatican City flag is constituted of two fields divided vertically, a yellow one next to the staff and the other white, and bears on the latter the tiara with the keys, all as seen in the model in Annex A of the present law.[49]

The original annexes of 1929 also bore black-and-white illustrations of the Vatican City coat of arms, seal, and flag (Fig. 3.12). Later annex printings incorporated slight alterations in the flag's tiara-and-keys emblem. These were replicated in the annexes of 2000 that provided color illustrations of the state arms as well as the flag (Fig. 3.13). In each version, the inscription on the flag annex reads:

> Official Flag of Vatican City State: Yellow and white fabric divided per pale, the white charged in the center with the crossed keys surmounted by the tiara. Yellow staff, striped with gold, surmounted by a lance adorned with a cravat of the same colors as the flag and fringed in gold.[50]

Of note, the flag annex portrays a square ceremonial flag with a unique staff, finial, and cravat, i.e., an infantry color. A lone corresponding specimen is carried by the Pontifical Swiss Guards for solemn events, such as their procession to St. Peter's Square for the papal blessing *urbi et orbi* ("to the city and world"). This occurs at Christmas and Easter, and when a new pope is elected (Fig. 3.14).[51] The Swiss Guards assemble with the Vatican infantry color, while opposite them, Italian troops from its military and police assemble with the Italian color (since Italy shares security responsibility for the square). Fanfares from the Pontifical and Italian anthems accompany the event.[52] Its staff is never dipped—lowered in honor of dignitaries—except during the Eucharistic consecration. When not in use, it is displayed in a cabinet in the officers' meeting room of the Swiss Guard's quarters in Vatican City.

The Vatican ceremonial flag was created around 1970, when the Palatine Honor Guard Corps was disbanded and its own color no longer represented the papal forces that assembled jointly. The square flag has two sewn stripes composed of heavy silk-like fabric, and a cravat with two tails divided vertically, white over yellow. Since 2012 its emblem follows the pattern of the 2000 constitution, but previously it followed the template in the 1929 constitution

Figure 3.14. Infantry Color, Christmas 2012, Piazza San Pietro

Figure 3.15. Infantry Color, ca. 1970–2009, Swiss Guard Quarters

Figure 3.16. Vatican state flag, 1938, Palazzo del Governatorato

Figure 3.17. Vatican state flag, Porta Sant'Anna, 1980

(Fig. 3.15).[53] Golden metal spiral braid surrounds its yellow staff, which is surmounted by a golden-bronze lance-head with an angel inside. At one time this finial also adorned some civic flagpoles within Vatican City.

State flags flown by Vatican buildings follow the basic constitutional design, but vary widely in details such as proportions, color shades, and emblem details. Though Vatican authorities presume that state flags be square, like the constitutional illustration[54] and early state flags (Fig. 3.16),[55] this is not regulated and occurs rarely today (Fig. 3.17).[56] Instead, since the 1960s or so, Vatican

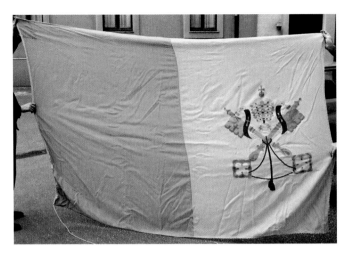

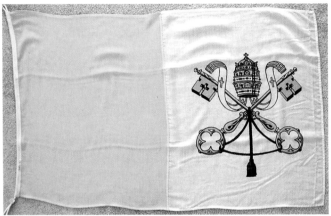

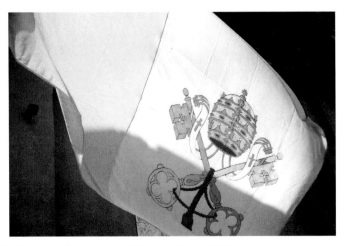

Figure 3.18. State flag variants, Vatican City, 1980s

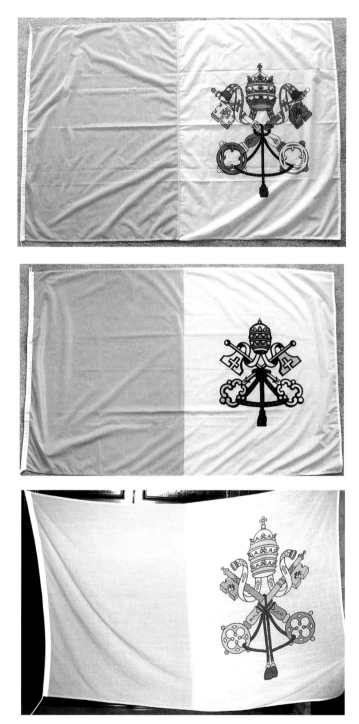

Figure 3.19. State flag variants, Vatican City, 2013

buildings fly oblong state flags that follow Italy's flag proportions (2:3), probably because they are mass-produced there (see Figs. 0.1–12). As shown here, other details also vary among different flagmakers (Figs. 3.18–19);[57] and in only one version does the emblem follow the actual constitutional template today (Fig. 3.20).[58] The shade of the yellow stripe ranges from the standard color "FM-yellow" (frequent) to orange-yellow (less frequent); and the emblem's precise colors, features, and size relative to the overall flag are subject to artistic license.

Such variations suggest that Vatican authorities could clarify the flag's details more precisely. Many nation-states issue detailed specifications that enhance their flag's dignity, prevent confusion, and provide clarity for production—e.g., defined proportions, precise color shades, and a standard emblem template. Such details exceed a constitution's scope. The flag's proportions deserve clarification (at least for Vatican sites) because the constitution's square infantry color might be considered distinct from state flags for public buildings. Indeed in the Papal States, Italy, and elsewhere, square military colors have often diverged from oblong civil and state flags. Moreover, Catholics worldwide also use the papal flag, although local flagmakers often rely on questionable sources (e.g., *Wikipedia*). Absent uniform specifications, Vatican flag reproductions will diverge widely, both at home and abroad.

Vatican Flag Customs

Little ceremony attends the papal flag at the Vatican, where its use is purposeful and unassuming (see Figs. 0.1–12). Unlike flags elsewhere, it is rarely raised or lowered to fanfare, erected indoors at offices, spread atop caskets, or subject to display codes, apart from appointed days to fly it.

Flag days are set forth by the Pontifical Commission for Vatican City State, its legislative body, and follow various Papal States precedents.[59] They include papal anniversaries, holy days of obligation, and state occasions (see Appendix V).[60] When a pope dies, flags fly at half-staff or bear mourning streamers, until the conclusion of the *novemdiales*, the nine days of mourning after his burial (Figs. 3.21–22).[61]

Within Vatican City the flag flies from a dozen buildings or so.[62] Typically, angled flagstaffs adorn windows or balconies near doorways. Vatican Gendarmes, Swiss Guards, or building porters manage its display.

Figure 3.20. State flag variant, 2016, Residenza Paulo VI (Extraterritorial Zone)

Figure 3.21. Vatican flag, 1939, at half-staff (death of Pius XI, Porta Sant'Anna, detail)

Figure 3.22. Vatican flag, 2005, with black streamer (death of John Paul II, Pont. Teut. Inst. of S. Maria dell'Anima)

The Holy See's extraterritorial zones also fly the Vatican flag. These non-contiguous enclaves lie beyond Vatican City and are governed by it—comprising about 2 square miles of Rome and its environs. They host over 100 pontifical entities, such as major basilicas, curial offices, educational establishments, and headquarters of religious orders. The Lateran Treaty granted diplomatic immunity to these sites, along with any future Holy See offices (and indeed, any Italian church when a pope visits).[63] Further pacts confirm this, resulting in 17 extra-territorial zones today. Nearly half adjoin Vatican City, others lie deeper into Rome, and two lie beyond it: the papal villas at Castel Gandolfo, and a large transmission site for Vatican Radio at Santa Maria di Galeria (see Appendix VI).[64]

Several other pontifical establishments in Rome have more limited privileges,[65] such as exemption from Italian taxes or seizure, and fly the papal flag more rarely. Foreign embassies to the Holy See, located throughout Rome, are also asked to fly their national flags on Vatican flag days.

Technically, Vatican City could also charter ships under its flag. Landlocked nations enjoy this right under the 1921 Barcelona Convention on Navigation. Indeed the Pontifical Commission for Vatican City State has published a decree "Concerning Maritime Navigation under the Flag of Vatican City State" and the Vatican owns dock space at the Mediterranean port of Civitavecchia. To date, however, the Vatican has not actualized its right, and the papal merchant register remains blank.[66]

Since the Holy See freely deploys the Vatican flag, a brief word on its structure is in order. Led by the pope, it governs the Catholic Church through four branches. An executive cabinet, the Roman Curia, directs church life and practice. A legislative-judicial arm codifies and adjudges Catholic canon law. A financial arm manages the See's investments and real estate, and offers banking services for Catholic entities. A civil arm, Vatican City's administration, governs the See's territory. All this is overseen by the Secretariat of State, along with the See's foreign relations. Its diplomatic posts deal with both the host church and state.

Papal diplomats fly the Vatican flag abroad at their apostolic nunciatures (where diplomatic relations exist) and apostolic delegations or other missions (where they do not); and it also flies at international organizations alongside those of other accredited states (alphabetically for "Holy See" in the local language).[67] This is of note because diplomacy is conducted in the name of the Holy See, not Vatican City State (except at global organizations of a purely temporal

Figure 3.23. Vatican flag, Apostolic Nunciature, Cuba

Figures 3.24–25. Vatican flag, Apostolic Nunciatures, Czech Republic (left) and United Kingdom (right)

nature);[68] and their two sovereignties are technically distinct. However, since papal authorities view the microstate as the sign and guarantee of the Holy See's sovereign status, the Vatican flag logically serves both entities, and is commonly referred to as "the papal flag," like its predecessors of old. Here it is shown at the Apostolic Nunciatures in Havana, Prague, and London (Figs. 3.23–25).[69]

The latter once flew a papal flag variant, to be examined presently.

Figure 3.26. Proposed Vatican flag design by Archbishop Bruno Heim

Figure 3.27. Vatican City State coat of arms

Figure 3.28. Holy See insignia (variant)

Figure 3.29. Roman Curia logo

Other Papal Flags and Arms

Irregular papal flags are also seen at times. Around 2000 the flag at the Apostolic Palace had a counterchanged border and obverse side, as featured in a news photo and television documentary.[70] Or sometimes the yellow-white stripes are overlaid by a centered papal emblem. Thus an erroneous Vatican flag flew at Amman airport in 1964, when Paul VI visited the Holy Land— the first modern pope to travel abroad: a vertical bicolor overlaid by a centered dark tiara-and-keys emblem within a ring. Later it was wrongly cited by a flag expert as the "Holy See flag".[71]

Another variant was proposed by an Italian flag expert in 1929. It surmounted the stripes with a small red oval shield bearing the tiara-and-keys emblem, reminiscent of Papal States infantry colors.[72] A striking design in this vein was also advocated by Archbishop Bruno Heim, a brilliant herald who designed the coats of arms for several popes. As papal emissary in London, he (and others elsewhere) flew a vertical bicolor surmounted by Vatican City's state arms, a red shield bearing the tiara-and-keys emblem (which he stylized; see Figs. 3.25–27).[73] Heim saw his design as more heraldic than the official flag with a silver key on a white field, which he deemed inapt because the two hues are heraldic correlates, and the emblem is less distinct.

Precisely for the same reason, in the constitution Vatican City's coat of arms places the emblem on a red shield instead of a white background (Fig. 3.27).[74] This stems from a 1929 study by Alberto Serafini, commissioned by the papal Secretariat of State.[75] He explained that heraldic aptitude precluded a white background for the tiara-and-keys emblem, and also cited the red color's antiquity; for in previous centuries the keys often appeared on a red shield or banner to represent the papacy (as examined previously).[76]

Usually Vatican City's coat of arms is employed by its state agents alone, and not by the Holy See's agents (unlike the Vatican flag, which is used by both). For insignia, Holy See agents use only the tiara-and-keys emblem (or the pontiff's own arms) on plaques, stationery, and the like, both in Rome and abroad.[77] Such use predates Vatican City's founding; and the Holy See website calls the insignia its own "coat of arms"—technically a misnomer, since it lacks customary heraldic elements such as a shield (Fig. 3.28).[78] The emblem is subject to wide artistic license, as in the Roman Curia logo (Fig. 3.29).[79]

Figures 3.30–32 (from top). Car pennants: Paul VI, John Paul II, Francis

Figure 3.33. Papal bicolor, Latin Patriarchate Chancellery Complex, Old Jerusalem

The fender pennants (*bandierine*) on papal automobiles are semi-official flags that often bear the pontiff's personal arms. Pius XI—the first to use cars—flew a yellow-white pennant with his arms bisecting the stripes.[80] This pattern was followed through Paul VI (Fig. 3.30).[81] John Paul II placed his arms on the white portion (Fig. 3.31), as did Benedict XVI. The latter also used an oblong yellow-white car flag with his arms on the white. For new popes the plain tiara-and-keys emblem appears on the pennant's white stripe, or the regular Vatican flag is used until a personal device is created. However, Pope Francis eschews car flags altogether, except when abroad, when his car flies the regular Vatican flag or pennant (Fig. 3.32).

Unofficial, handheld flags in both Rome and Poland during the pontificate of John Paul II bore his own coat of arms on the white stripe. Similar flags bearing the arms of successive popes have appeared in various places, but never fly from Vatican buildings.

During a vacant see, the Vatican flag does not change, contrary to occasional myth, but the papal insignia does: the tiara is replaced by the ceremonial umbrella of the Roman Church—representing the *camerlengo* (cardinal-chamberlain) who administers the vacant see.[82] This emblem appears on special coins, stamps, medallions, and the like—but not flags.

A further myth arises from the distinct sovereignties held by Vatican City and the Holy See: namely, that each uses a different version of the papal flag (such as reversing the gold and silver keys). This is not accurate. Only one version of the Vatican flag is official, and it serves the affairs of both Vatican City and its holder, the Holy See.[83]

At times papal flags lack any emblem at all. Indeed, throughout the Catholic world a plain bicolor of yellow and white (usually vertical) often flies in honor of the papacy or Catholicism (Fig. 3.33).[84] Such flags lack legal sanction but enjoy a simple, low-cost appeal. Moreover, as early as 1929 a Roman myth held that the Holy See's extraterritorial properties were to fly such a bicolor instead of the regular Vatican flag.[85] On the contrary, Vatican City's governorate directs such sites to fly the regular Vatican flag.[86]

Finally, large draperies with the pontiff's personal arms adorn windows or balconies from which he addresses open-air gatherings at the Vatican or Castel Gandolfo.

Figure 3.34. Swiss Guard Color, Gregory XVI

Figure 3.35. Swiss Guard Color, Pius IX

Figure 3.36a. Swiss Guard Color (obverse), Pius IX in exile

Figure 3.36b. Swiss Guard Color (reverse), Pius IX in exile

Armed Corps

The Pontifical Swiss Guard Corps, which has guarded popes continuously since 1506, carries a striking flag based on elements from previous flags. For some centuries these flags included stripes in the blue-red-yellow colors of the Medici popes—the same colors which today are reflected in their dress uniform.[87]

Striped flags appear early. In the 1500s two frescos show a striped flag bearing the papal coat of arms. A fresco from the era of Pius IV (1560–65) shows it with twenty horizontal stripes of red alternating with yellow, emblazoned with the papal arms of the Medici. It is shown with red, blue, and yellow stripes in a fresco showing the coronation of Sixtus V in 1585.[88] The order of the stripes is uncertain, as is their number. In a 1736 painting, a flag with nine horizontal stripes and bearing the papal arms, is shown flying from the pope's Quirinal Palace, and is also confirmed by documents later in the century—apparently in the order blue-yellow-red[89] (see also Fig. 1.24).

From at least the early 1800s, the nine stripes instead appeared in the thrice-repeated order of blue-red-yellow, and bore the pope's arms at the top and those of the commander at the bottom (as in Fig. 3.34, showing the arms of Gregory XVI). The earliest such flag preserved at the Guard's Vatican quarters probably dates from the reign of Pius VIII (1829–30)—although his arms were subsequently painted over with those of his successors, Gregory XVI (1831–46) and Pius IX (1846–78), whose arms remain. It is preserved today at the Guard's quarters (Fig. 3.35); the bottom section is lost.[90] Photos of the era show it flying in Piazza San Pietro (see Fig. 1.25).

A second Swiss Guard flag from the reign of Pius IX is also preserved in their quarters (Fig. 3.36).[91] It was apparently used during his exile in Gaeta (1848–50), where he blessed it. It is a square flag with only three horizontal stripes: cobalt blue, red, and golden-yellow. On the obverse, the center stripe bears Pius's arms surmounted by the tiara-and-keys emblem, and within a gold wreath. The top stripe bears (at the hoist) the Swiss arms surrounded by the gold motto SCHWEIZERISCHE EIDGENOSSENSCHAFT (Swiss Confederation) within a green wreath, and (at the fly) a gold wreath. The gold wreath was designed to surround the captain commander's coat of arms, but they were never added because a definitive command was not then granted. The reverse of this flag is the same except that in place of Pius's arms, the tiara-and-keys emblem (with both keys gold) appears beneath the arched inscription in gold, GUARDIA SVIZZERA PONTIFICIA.[92]

Figure 3.37. Swiss Guard Color,
Leo XIII

Figure 3.38. Swiss Guard Color,
Pius X & Commander von Schauensee

Figure 3.39. Swiss Guard Color, 1913
pattern, Pius X & Commander Repond

Figure 3.40. Swiss Guard Color,
2015– , Francis & Commander Graf

Under Leo XIII (1878–1903), the flag changed to horizontal stripes of white-red-gold (i.e., with white instead of blue). This was due to confusion over the faded shade of blue being proposed, which appeared white; but Leo saw the combination as a symbolic mingling of the papal and Swiss colors, and authorized it anyway. The flag is preserved at the Guard's quarters (Fig. 3.37).[93]

Under Pius X (1903–1914) the flag returned to the blue-red-gold motif, with his coat of arms at the top and those of the commander at the bottom.

That flag is also preserved at the Guard's quarters, bearing the arms of Commander Leopold Meyer von Schauensee (1901–1910) (Fig. 3.38).[94]

The current pattern of the Swiss Guard flag was introduced by Commander Jules Repond (1910–1921), who also refined their uniform. It was designed by Robert Durrer, a Swiss archivist, whose sketch was approved by the papal Secretariat of State on 1 November 1913. Subsequently, the actual flag was produced at a Swiss convent in time for its blessing on 5 May 1914. In that year it is pictured bearing the arms of Pius X (Fig. 3.39).[95]

The flag's design and size is codified in the Swiss Guard Rules.[96] It is square and bears a large white cross, recalling flags carried by Swiss troops in centuries past. The resulting quarters bear the arms of the reigning pope and those of the Guard's founder, Pope Julius II (1503–1513), counterposed with stripes in the colors of the Guard—red, gold, and blue. These also appear in their dress uniform, and recall the colors of Pope Clement VII, who was saved by the Guard at great sacrifice during the sack of Rome in 1527. The commander's arms appear in the center, encircled by a green wreath and mounted upon a background in the colors of the Swiss canton from which he hails.

The flag is altered upon selection of a new pope or unit commander.[97] The current version was blessed on 1 May 2015 by the papal Secretary of State, Cardinal Pietro Parolin. It bears the arms of Pope Francis along with those of a new commander, Christoph Graf of Lucerne (Fig. 3.40).[98] Under Francis two further changes have appeared in the flag. Since May 2013 his arms are rendered with the use of a miter instead of a tiara (which was not done under Benedict XVI even though his arms initiated the use of the miter); and since May 2015 the corner stripes follow the same order (whereas previously the second quarter reversed the red and blue stripes).

In some cases a transition period is too brief for a new flag to be introduced. This transpired during the pontificate of John Paul I (1978) and the command of Colonel Alois Estermann (1998), both of whom suffered untimely deaths. In John Paul's case no flag was produced; in Estermann's case one was completed but never used.[99] The fabric is always silk damask, the same material as the famous "Julian banners" that were conferred upon Swiss cantons in 1512 to acknowledge their loyalty to the pope during his wars against France.[100] The flagstaff has often been surmounted by a spearhead finial bearing an image of the Guard's patron, St. Nikolaus von Flüe. A yellow and white streamer hangs from the top of the pike as a commendation for service to the papacy, granted after the restructuring of the various Vatican security forces by Paul VI.

Figures 3.41–42. Swiss Guard color, Bronze Door entry, color of Pius X (left) & Benedict XVI (right)

Figure 3.43. Swiss Guard color, St. Peter's Square, Pius XI

Figure 3.44. Swiss Guard oath, ca. 1960

On Vatican flag days, the Swiss Guard flag is posted near the Bronze Doors adjoining St. Peter's Square—usually indoors, rarely outdoors (Figs. 3.41–43).[101] On 6 May it is carried to Cortile di San Damaso for the annual induction of new recruits. There it becomes the focus of the swearing-in known as the *Fahneneid* (flag oath), as each new recruit grasps the banner, raises his right hand, and pledges to protect the pontiff (Fig. 3.44).[102] Later the flag is carried to the Swiss Guard's barracks courtyard, where the Vatican and Swiss flags are displayed, along with those of the Swiss cantons. When not in use, the flag hangs in the commander's office.

The Vatican City State Gendarme Corps received a distinctive unit flag on 27 September 2008.[103] Designed by Cardinal Andrea Cordero Lanza di Montezemolo, its pattern resembles the Pontifical Gendarme Corps color retired in 1970 (i.e., a blue field with the pontiff's arms, Fig. 3.45).[104] The new flag uses a lighter blue and bears the Vatican state arms instead of the pontiff's (Fig. 3.46).[105] The shield is stylized as a red heptagon edged in yellow. The arms are framed by golden branches, at whose base is the motto FIDES ET VIRTUS. The flag is hemmed in a gold border and bears gold fringe. Its staff—colored spirally in yellow and white—bears a statuette finial of St. Michael the Archangel. The corps also carries an oblong Vatican parade flag fringed in gold. It has a spirally-colored staff (yellow-white) whose finial is the tiara-and-keys emblem.

Figures 3.45–46. Gendarmerie, ca. 1950 (top) & since 2008 (bottom)

Figure 3.47. Poland, 1979, Visit of John Paul II

Figure 3.48. Italian Parliament, 2002, Visit of John Paul II

Papal Flags Today

As the Petrine keys span the millennia, the pope's modern colors have now begun their third century, having first appeared in 1808, in a yellow-and-white papal cockade opposing Napoleon's seizure of Rome. Born that year from the pope's symbolic protest, the colors inspired an enduring legacy. Although the Papal States have passed, their yellow-white flags became a persistent sign of papal sovereignty throughout the European revolutions of the 1800s—a claim codified today in the Lateran Accords of 1929. It was none too soon. With the rise of fascism and the Nazi occupation of Rome, the papal flag quietly reminded the world once again that other empires would never usurp the papacy's mission.

Indeed, under John Paul II the reverse seemed to unfold. Upon returning to his native land for his first visit, the Marxist red flag, which usually accompanied Poland's in town squares and city centers, was replaced by the papal flag (Fig. 3.47).[106] Though its display was brief, it heralded the impending peaceful downfall of communism in Europe, aided and abetted by the pope. As a new millennium beckoned, the Vatican flag greeted many such symbolic moments, flying alongside scores of national flags in distant lands as popes pursued dialogue and understanding.

Figure 3.49. Scotland, 2010, Visit of Benedict XVI

Figure 3.50. U.S.A., 2013, Election of Pope Francis, Cathedral of Ss. Peter & Paul, Indianapolis

Important among these are its historic displays at the United Nations, where popes appealed for "war no more"; in the Holy Land on either side of disputed borders; at the Italian parliament for a papal visit that a century earlier was unthinkable (Fig. 3.48);[107] and in lands of every creed and race. When Benedict XVI retired to Castel Gandolfo's papal palace in 2013, the closing of its doors and the lowering of its flag signaled the first resignation of a pope in six centuries.[108] Truly, the papal flag has come of age as a symbol of the Sovereign Pontiff, and the moral suasion of his global office ("soft power").

In the world of symbols, flags are preeminent; and among them, the Vatican's is unique in two ways. First, no other national flag is yellow and white. These distinctive colors reflect the Petrine keys of gold (yellow) and silver (white)—and thus the pope's authority to "bind and loose" the communion of faith (see Matthew 16). Second, and paradoxically, the Vatican flag is among the most widely flown globally, despite serving a microstate—for it symbolizes Catholic identity worldwide. It often appears at Catholic churches, schools, offices, and charities, with the host nation's banner. When a pope travels, his colors are fêted by throngs of well-wishers (Fig. 3.49);[109] and when a pope is elected, yellow-white bunting adorns church lintels in every land (Fig. 3.50)[110]—a striking legacy, indeed.

As the modern papacy has evolved globally, so has its flag. With this book, its deserving story is finally told. Amazed by its display at a remote Irish farmstead, G. K. Chesterton once called it "a tower of crowns and a parade of keys";[111] for it points to a kingdom that embraces all creation—even its remotest corners—striving toward the fullness of God. Unlike other flags, few have died for this one; but many have labored faithfully for the shepherd it represents, or the peaceful mission of the church that he heads. Perhaps in that light, all people of good will can honor the Bishop of Rome, and the banner with his keys.

Notes, Chapter 3

1. Kertzer, *Prisoner of the Vatican*, passim.

2. Andreotti, insert, p. VI.

3. *Roma nelle fotografie della Raccolta Ceccarius*, p. 92, reports that its flag was "discovered" in 1920. But which flag? Might the jack have been preserved separately from its ensign (see Fig. 1.15)? If so, one might surmise that it flew from the moored ship when Civitavecchia surrendered, and was subsequently struck in favor of its ensign. Indeed Ziggioto reports an 1876 chart showing only two flags for the papal yacht: the former Papal States war ensign (white with the effigies of Peter and Paul, surmounted by the tiara-and-keys emblem) and the former Holy See ensign (white with a crucifix) used to signify the personal presence of the pope—but not the jack ("Le bandiere degli stati italiani", part II, p. 98; also part I, p. 123, n. 30).

4. For the naval flags, see Figs. 1.15 & 1.19 and Appendix III, for Museum Deposits at the Vatican Historical Museum. The ship was donated to a boys' school later in the decade (Bouquet; Alvarez, p. 258).

5. References to a papal flag at the Bronze Doors likely concern the Swiss Guard flag, as evidenced by photos or illustrated accounts: Pesci, p. 16; and "El Jubileo de León XIII". See also Hart, p. 189 (who references white and yellow stripes—found in the Guard flag under Leo XIII); Special Correspondent, p. 784. Krieg, p. 448, reports that the Swiss Guard flag flew there on special occasions from the pontificate of Gregory XVI. However during papal conclaves the marshal's flag is reported there: cf. Richards, p. 116.

6. *Civiltà Cattolica*, anno 59, vol. 2, p. 108 (1908 in Cortile San Damaso). "Prince Rospigliosi Dead" (1915). "Greet Pope on Name Day" (1924). "Pope Pius 67 Years Old" (1924). "Soundings by Mussolini" (1928—mentions a bicolor). "Pope Announces Accord with Italy" (February 1929 in Cortile San Damaso—mentions the tiara-and-keys emblem). "Pope 72 Years Old Today" (May 1929).

7. Illustration from "*Päpstliche Flagge—Drapeau Pontifical*", illustrated color postcard, H. Guggenheim & Co., Zurich, no. 10489, author's archives, undated (publisher flourished in the early 20th century; antique postcard dealers at eBay online auctions report the flag series dates from 1906–1919; a postmarked version in author's digital archives dates from 1913).

8. An early case in point was the rupture of the Holy See's relations with France, occasioned by the exchange of state visits between its President and the King of Italy, in October 1903 (Paris) and April 1904 (Rome). During the latter, Pius X refused to meet French President Émile Loubet, because no Catholic nation's head of state had previously visited the Italian monarchs who had "usurped" the pope's temporal sovereignty. The message conveyed by Pius's refusal was likely amplified by flying a proto-national bicolor flag at the apostolic palace—apparently for the first time since 1870 (at least officially). Indeed prior to 1870 there is no record of such a flag at the palace (although the Swiss Guard flag flew at the Bronze Doors, either indoors or outdoors).

9. For Papal States forts, see p. 53; for the 1929 design process, see p. 96.

10. Cf. "Vatican: King Victor Emmanuel III and Queen Elena arriving for meeting with Pope Pius XI", Vatican City, 5 December 1929, British Pathé video footage at 2:22 in Cortile di San Damaso, retrieved online (21 June 2018) at: <www.britishpathe.com/video/ VLVAAKZ74ZTW316ZSSDLX4M5P558U-VATICAN-KING-VICTOR-EMMANUEL- III-AND-QUEEN-ELENA-ARRIVING-FOR/query/Emmanuel>. Class photos show the proto-national papal flag at the Pontifical North American College, Rome: 1930, 1931, 1932,

1933, 1940, 1942, 1944. An Italian encyclopedia also carried it into the 1930s: Rangoni-Machiavelli, pl. 2 (separate editor). It flew in May 1929 at Montecassino Abbey in honor of its 14th centenary celebrations; cf. "La processione religiosa nell'abbazia di Montecassino in occassione del 14° centenario", Giornale Luce A0329, video footage at 0:42 retrieved online (21 June 2018) at: <www.youtube.com/watch?v=6JaBn8px45o>.

11. "La bandera pontificia en Buenos Aires". For more on papal diplomats, see p 93.

12. Illustration from "Waiting for the Holy Father [i.e., Pius X]—throngs of the faithful in the Court of San Damaso in the Vatican, Rome". Underwood & Underwood Publishers, Arlington NJ (USA), no. H 38688, registered with the Library of Congress 1 December 1903 (entry 76440), author's archives. A similar photo (with the emblem obscured) is titled, "The Holy Father is speaking! Eager throngs in the Court of San Damaso in the Vatican". Stereoview photography (dual stereoscopic photos), Underwood & Underwood Publishers, Arlington, New Jersey (USA), nos. H 38710–H 38714, original photos registered with the Library of Congress 1 December 1903 (entry 76409–76413), author's archives. Cf. Catalogue of Title Entries, p. 839/1009. A fixed flagstaff does not seem attested before Pius X, and may have been erected due to his regular public audiences in the courtyard.

13. Several from the era of Pius XI are in the author's archives. "Accademia Poliglotta—Vaticano—8.VI.1922", commemorative photo by G. Felici, Rome. "La solenna udienza concessa dal S. Padre alle 10.000 rappresentanti della G.F.C.I. [Gioventù Femminile Cattolica Italiana] in occasione del IV Congresso Nazionale nel decennio di fondazione—Roma 15 Luglio 1928", Photo postcard no. 25549, no publisher listed. Also, P & A Photos, "The Pope's Own Feast Day", London Bureau, 24 May 1929 [Feast of St. Neres and Achilles], FEL 200368.

14. "Roma—Vaticano—Giuramento della Guardia Palatina", black and white photo-postcard, STA, no. 8430, undated, showing the induction of Palatine Guard recruits; the flag's folds obscure the emblem (author's collections). A postmarked version dates from 1910; antique postcard dealers date the card ca. 1910–1920. "Automobili Pontifici nel Cortile di S. Damaso", black and white photo edited by G. Felici, shows the flag flying alongside automobiles with diplomatic plates, perhaps ca. 1925 (author's collections), also online (retrieved 21 June 2018) at: <www.romasparita.eu/foto-roma-sparita/106001/chiesa-san-damaso>.

15. Illustration from Zaricor Flag Collection, Santa Cruz, California, no. ZFC0222, 16 July 2005, retrieved online (18 March 2005) at: <www.flagcollection.com/collection/photos/maxi/ZFC0222001.jpg>. The label "Pontifical States military color" was provided by Dr. Whitney Smith of the Flag Research Center in Winchester, Massachusetts. Whatever its original location of use, it presumably dates from the Roman Question period. Flag acquired in 1912 by the De Young Museum, San Francisco, from William P. Burke, and in 1997 by Ben Zaricor for the Zaricor Flag Collection. The flag measures 107 x 152 cm (42 x 60 in.). See also online (23 July 2018) at: www.flagcollection.com/cmsmedia//themes/Italy/ZFC0222001.jpg, www.flagcollection.com/resourcesstaticcontent.php?CollectionHTMLZone_Code=resources_heart_italy, and www.flagcollection.com/itemsummary.php?CollectionItem_ID=218.

16. Illustration from author's collections. Flag acquired by author in 2007 from belongings of an unidentified cardinal whose goods were being disposed by his grand-nephew through an antique dealer in Bassano, near Brescia; 142 x 140 cm (56 x 55 in.).

17. Illustration from Barrett, p. 96b; Giovanni Battista Montini studied there from 1903–1914. The flag is square in format and appears to be at half-staff.

18. Illustration from author's collections. Flag acquired by author in 2017 from an online auction in Baffadi, Italy, 140 x 140 cm (55 x 55 in.). The emblem resembles that found in the Rupoli Papal Fort Flag (Fig. 2.21).

19. The location may be the Palatine Guard Quarters, since their monogram appears on the trumpet banners, and they used ceremonial rifles. The three young guards appear to wear a service uniform of the corps: cf. the website of their successor association, online (retrieved 21 June 2018) at: <pietroepaolo.org/incontro18.html>. Major Peter Hasler, Swiss Guard archivist, suggests the man sitting between the two clergymen might be Alois Hirschbühl, the Swiss Guard commander from 1921 to 1935 (email to Rev. Richard Kunst, 1 March 2018).

20. Cf. Rosenfeld (1883), pl. 11 (1883—"Päpstliche Flagge: Hausflagge"). Martin et al., pl. 2 (1896—"flag of the Holy See"). *Grand Larousse Illustré* (1929). Ziggioto, "Le bandiere degli stati italiani", part II, p. 98. Less likely is that the former white fort flag with the papal arms remained in use, although some flag sources report it anachronistically: cf. Rosenfeld (1883), pl. 11, with arms of Leo XIII.

21. "ROMA—Anno Santo 1925—Pius XI in the Vatican Gardens", illustrated (watercolor signed "Ellero") multilingual postcard, no. 4441–5, A. Scrocchi, Milano. Opposite the papal banners are similar banners of red and yellow—the civic colors of Rome.

22. See pp. 65–67 & 71. Pius XI greeted and kissed the yellow-white Palatine Guard flag after his election—a harbinger of his intent to restore a temporal state: cf. Usai, pp. 109–121; Governatorato, p. 403.

23. "Drapeaux pontificaux", pp. 100 & 102, presents a standard with six-pointed stars and the coat of arms of Pius X, but this is uncorroborated elsewhere. News photos and footage (author's archives) shows a Noble Guardsman holding a standard bearing the umbrella-keys insignia when Pius XII took possession of the Lateran Basilica (1939) and upon the coronation of John XXIII at St. Peter's Basilica (1958). Though misnamed, the standard is pictured online (retrieved 21 June 2018) at <marcellinonews.blogspot.com/2012/10/lepanto-bandiera-pontificia.html>.

24. Richards, p. 116. Wire photos, author's archives: International News Photos, 22 February 1939, no. F0868962; and Associated Press Photo, 19 June 1963, no. 07022704293. The large flag was square and disposed vertically, bearing the marshal's princely arms, attached to a staff which was mounted diagonally to a wall or balustrade. One such flag is preserved by the Vatican Historical Museum (unnumbered; flag of Prince Chigi della Rovere). The hereditary position belonged to the Chigi family in modern times, but was abolished with the restructuring of the Pontifical Household on 28 March 1968.

25. See pp. 59, 90–91, and also "La bandera pontificia en Buenos Aires". *Memoria que el Ministro de Estado*, "Santa Sede", p. 3, records the apostolic delegate in Lima, announcing the flag at half-staff in 1878 upon the death of Pius IX. Lafort, p. 728, reports a papal flag flying at France's nunciature to honor the state visit of the Russian Czar in 1896, "for the first time since 1870", but it is unclear whether the reference implies use of a flag before the fall of Papal Rome (cf. also *Semaine religieuse*, 1896, p. 583). Pierconti, p. 596f., also reports a flag there in 1903 upon the death of Leo XIII and the elevation of Pius X (cf. also *Semaine religieuse*, 1903, p. 229). Portugal's nunciature hoisted a papal flag for protection during local unrest in October 1910 (cf. "Religious Orders Exiled").

26. "The Papal Embassadors [sic]". "Pope Says Glory will Shine Here". "Papal Flag to Fly First Time at Sea [sic]". "Liner to Fly Papal Flag".

27. Museo Civico del Risorgimento di Modena, No. 792, 41 x 38.5 cm (16 x 15" in.), ca. 1900–1925. Retrieved online (18 June 2018) at: <bbcc.ibc.regione.emilia-romagna.it/pater/loadcard.do?id_card=67603>.

28. Scott, pp. 49–57. Pidoux, "Le drapeau pontifical".

29. Cf. flag catalogs of the American Flag Company from about 1912 (p. 128) and 1916 (p. 106, anachronistic arms of Pius X); and Annin & Company from 1914 (Annin & Co. *Makers of Fine Flags...* [New York, Annin, 1914]).

30. Commercial flag catalogue, 1897 (Cincinnati: The National Flag Company, 1897), p. 25, bearing the arms of Leo XIII.

31. The yellow-white flag is fringed and bears the arms of Pius XI on the white stripe. It was exhibited at festivities marking the 80th anniversary of Vatican City State in 2009. Presumably held by the Vatican, its provenance and use are unclear to the author—and it may have been a gift of some kind: cf. J. P. Sonnen, *Orbis Catholicus* Blog, 12, 13, & 15 February 2009, retrieved online (21 June 2018) via <orbiscatholicus.blogspot.com/2009/02>; and email to author, 7 July 2009.

32. Illustration from "Bandiera dell'Italia e del Vaticano alla loggia di Palazzo Chigi: 12/02/1929", photo, 12 February 1929, Archivio Storico Istituto Luce, Rome, author's archives, retrieved online (20 November 2005) at <www.archivioluce.it/galleria/multimedia. asp?documentID=1059>. The photo was popularized in a contemporary postcard inscribed, "La Conciliazione fra l'Italia e il Vaticano: la folla in Piazza Colonna acclama il Duce; le due bandiere al Palazzo Chigi". Sites displaying the papal colors included Palazzo Colonna, Palazzo Massimo, Castel Sant'Angelo, St. Peter's Basilica, and many buildings along the Borgo Pio: cf. "Patti Lateranensi", in *Riassunto Anno 1929*, retrieved online (9 August 2010) at <www.cronologia.it/storia/a1929h.htm>. Cf. Williamson, p. 33.

33. Illustration from news photo, 11 February 1929, Argo Agenzia Fotografica, Milan, author's archives, inscribed: "L'accordo fra lo Stato Italiano e la Santa Sede avvenuto in Roma il 11/2/1929. La bandiera papale che dal 1870 non venne più esposta ricompare oggi unita a quella dello Stato al Palazzo della Posta Centrale colla bandiera Papale e quelle dello Stato". The bicolor is white over yellow.

34. "Bandiera Pontificia", Archivio Segreto Vaticano, *Segretaria di Stato*, Anno 1929, Rubr. 240, fascicolo 1, folios 236–330.

35. "Bandiera Pontificia", ASV, *Segr. Stato*, An. 1929, Rubr. 240, fasc. 1, folios 260, 261, 263, 264.

36. "Bandiera Pontificia", ASV, *Segr. Stato*, An. 1929, Rubr. 240, fasc. 1, folios 243, 246, 252, 253. The Italian description refers to a square yellow-white vertical bicolor attached to a yellow staff with a lance-head finial bearing a yellow-white cravat.

37. Illustration from Vigevano, pl. 1; cf. pp. 75–76 (published in 1920). Repeated in Fig. 2.16.

38. Pagliucchi, 'Bandiere pontificie di stato e militari,' in "Bandiera Pontificia", ASV, *Segr. Stato*, An. 1929, Rubr. 240, fasc. 1, folios 269–273 (typewritten) & 279–284 (handwritten). Supplements include papal flag decrees from 1825 (maritime ensigns) and 1855 (award ensigns), and several illustrations. Vigevano seems to be a key study source, since Pagliucchi appends his illustration of the final Papal States infantry color (Vigevano, pl. 1).

39. His father was Eugenio Pagliucchi; cf. Pagliucchi, *I castellani*: vol. 1, pt. 1 (dedication page); and vol. 2, pt. 2 (i.e., tome 3, pp. 193–194).

40 Illustration from "Bandiera Pontificia", ASV, *Segr. Stato*, An. 1929, Rubr. 240, fasc. 1, folios 285–287 (all rights reserved, used with permission). Flagmakers attested to their manufacture of plain bicolors and/or the proto-national design with the emblem bisecting the stripes, whether vertical or horizontal (folios 260–264).

41. "Bandiera Pontificia", ASV, *Segr. Stato*, An. 1929, Rubr. 240, fasc. 1, folio 303. Its similarity to the Noble Guard color is noted in folio 308.

42. See Appendix IV, p. 41, and Fig. 2.8.

43. See pp. 11 & 59.

44. *Atti del Sommo Pontifice Pio IX*, vol. II, pp. 6–10: treaty between the Papal States and Tuscany governing "reciprocal equal treatment" of ships bearing their respective flags in the other's ports.

45. See Appendix I and Chapter 2 ("Yellow-White Ensigns", "Infantry Colors", "Fort, State, & Civil Flags", "Civic & Palatine Guard"). Zara, p. 136; Ziggioto, "Le bandiere degli stati italiani", part I, p. 117. Some sources erroneously suggest that the Papal States civil ensign was flown on land in the 19th century: cf. Tabet, pl. 4–7, followed by Smith, *Flags*, p. 57. Geoffrey Briggs, in an addition (Plate VIII) to Galbreath's Papal Heraldry, erroneously claimed it was "adopted as the Papal Banner by Pope Pius VII in 1809".

46. "Legge fondamentale dello Stato della Città del Vaticano", 7 June 1929. It was entered into a supplement of the Holy See's gazette on 7 June along with several other legal provisions; but the whole supplement was only released on 8 June (including one provision entered that day). Although article 21 provided that the constitution entered into force upon publication, 7 June is considered its effective date.

47. See "Credenziali presentate da S. E. Borgoncini Duca a S. M. il Re: La bandiera del Vaticano sventola su Villa Maria Pia", 8 July 1929, Archivo Luce, photo retrieved online (21 June 2018) at: <fondoluce.archivioluce.com/LuceUnesco/avanzata/scheda/foto/IL0000026680/12/La-bandiera-del-Vaticano-sventola-su-Villa-Maria-Pia.html>. Also, "Il nunzio apostolico si reca al Quirinale per presentare le credenziali al re", video retrieved online (21 June 2018) at: <www.youtube.com/watch?v=a2IMRAYAZ8s>.

48. "Legge fondamentale dello Stato della Città del Vaticano", updated version promulgated 26 November 2000, published 1 February 2001, effective 22 February 2001, retrieved online (21 June 2018) via: <www.vatican.va/news_services/press/documentazione/docs_index_en.htm>. Cf. "New Fundamental Law Promulgated for Vatican City State".

49. Article 19 (1929 version), and article 20 (2000 version).

50. Illustrations and citation from Annex A in both the 1929 and 2000 versions. The caption "*bandiera ufficiale*" parallels those at the bottom of the design drafts of 1929 (Fig. 3.11). See also Becker, "Vatican Flags", p. 217–218; Becker, "The Flag of Vatican City", Fig. A; Arias Pérez, pp. 21–27.

51. Illustration from the Swiss Guard website, retrieved online (10 March 2013) at: <www.swissguard.va/uploads/pics/25.12.2012_0406.jpg>

52. Regarding the papal anthem, see the respective websites of the Vatican State and the Holy See, retrieved online (21 June 2018) at: <www.vaticanstate.va/content/vaticanstate/en/stato-e-governo/note-generali/inno.html> and <www.vatican.va/news_services/press/documentazione/documents/sp_ss_scv/inno/inno_scv_testo_it.html>.

53. Illustrations from Pontifical Swiss Guards. The flag measured 116 cm (46 in.) square, and was double-sided—such that the silver key handle appeared on the dexter on both sides of the flag. The image shown here was adjusted by the author from a reverse image. The emblem followed the format found in the *Legge Fondamentale* of 1929 which is slightly different from that of 2000. The keys were embroidered in metallic gold and silver thread, connected by a golden cord. The tiara was white with golden crowns on which were embroidered red jewels—but not on the bands at their bases. The tiara's infulae were gold

on their obverse and silver on their reverse, and its inner lining (visible at its base) was white. (Swiss Guard Major Peter Hasler, emails to author, 17 May 2005, and 30 March 2009 with photos.) From Easter 2009 to Christmas 2012 the silk flag was unused because of wear. Instead an oblong polyester flag (100 x 150 cm [39 x 59 in.]) with a lemon-yellow stripe, as shown at the top of Fig. 3.19) without a cravat was attached to the ceremonial staff, which is approximately 2.6 m (8.5 ft.) tall (author's observations on site, April 2009).

54. Archbishop Paul J. Marcinkus, President of the Pontifical Commission for Vatican City State, asserted that Vatican state flags should be square like the infantry color in the constitutional illustration (letter to Whitney Smith, 14 January 1986, Flag Research Center files). Cf. also, Ceresa. However, since the Vatican flag design process in 1929 incidentally employed a square infantry color illustration as a draft template, it is not clear to this author whether the designer had state flags for public buildings in mind: see pp. 95–96.

55. Illustration from *L'Osservatore Romano* photo no. 397798, 10 July 1938, captioned "Piazalle del Governatorato: Annual feast of the Palatine Guard. Msgr. Amleto Tondini reads the 'Guards Prayer'; in the group to the left, Msgr. Montini, Sostituto of the Secretariat of State, who presided over the solemn ceremony; and the commanders of the Armed Pontifical Corps". This author's archives include other photos of square Vatican state flags: 8 July 1929 at Italy's new papal nunciature, Villa Maria Pia ("Credenziali presentate da S. E. Borgoncini Duca a S. M. il Re", Archivo Luce); 11 February 1932 in Cortile di San Damaso (Mussolini visits Pius XI, Critical Past); February 1939 at the Holy Office (Death of Pius XI, British Pathe); 10 February 1939 at the Cancello Sant'Anna (Death of Pius XI, Vedo News Service); 10 October 1958 at Castel Gandolfo's Pontifical Palace (Death of Pius XII, British Pathe and Associated Press.

56. Illustration from Aled Betts (Bettsy1970), "Papal Swiss Guard, Vatican, 1980", *Flickr*, retrieved online (9 August 2010) at <www.flickr.com/photos/bettsy1970/1806328542>.

57. Illustrations from author's photos while present in Rome; the more recent templates reflect emblems appearing at the Holy See's current or former website (as in Figs. 3.13 & 3.28–29).

58. Illustration from Uli Deck/dpa, licensed online (July 2018) at: <www.alamy.com/stock-photo-a-flag-with-the-coat-of-arms-of-vatican-city-waves-in-vatican-city-117429630.html>.

59. *Giornale militare officiale*, pp. 839–845 (fortress flag protocols). Vatican custom probably mirrored that of Italy, where public buildings likewise flew the tricolor on appointed days— both in 1929 and today.

60. Cf. Ceresa; and Archbishop Paul J. Marcinkus, President, Pontifical Commission for Vatican City State, letter to Monsignor M. Charles Murphy in response to author's inquiry, 27 September 1983. Protocol no. 122537.

61. Illustration in Figure 3.21 from Foto Vedo, Rome, 10 February 1939: "Subito dopo la comunicazione ufficiale della morte di Papa Pio XI, in tutti gli edifici vaticani è stata esposta la bandiera pontificia a mezz'asta, in segno di lutto. Bandiera a mezz'asta negli edifici che costeggiano l'ingresso al Cortile di S.Anna"; full photo online (2 July 2018) at: <vatflag.tripod.com/1939-halfstaff.jpg>. Illustration in Figure 3.22 from user Anthony Majanlahti (antmoose) at flickr.com, retrieved online (21 June 2018) at: <www.flickr.com/photos/antmoose/8353076>. Cf. also the death of Pius XII at Castel Gandolfo, in "A Simple End to a Pope's Splendid Life", Life 45:16 (20 October 1958), p. 23 ("Lowered papal flag at half mast was fixed in place at 4:03 a.m."); as available online (21 June 2018) at: <images.google.com/hosted/life/0308a90530b4538d.html> and <www.gettyimages.com/license/50578038>.

62. The papal flag routinely flies atop the Vatican Museums and at entry points like the Teutonic College (technically extraterritorial) or Porta Sant'Anna, where it flies from the Swiss Guard Commander's apartment and St. Anne's Church. Deeper within it flies from the Gendarmerie Quarters, the Fire Station, Vatican Radio headquarters, the Governorate, Palazzo San Carlo, Casa Santa Marta, the Gendarmerie Command, the Judiciary, the Canonicate Palace, and the courtyards of the Swiss Guard as well as the Apostolic Palace (Cortile di San Damaso). Other buildings occasionally fly it too, especially when the pope visits them.

63. Cf. the Lateran Treaty, 11 February 1929, articles 13–15 and the tables in Annex 2. A more or less comprehensive map is available at *OpenStreetMap* ("Relation: Extraterritorial area of the Holy See [6474878])", retrieved online (21 June 2018) at: <www.openstreetmap.org/relation/6474878>.

64. The Holy See compiled a list of current extraterritorial sites ("Elenco degi enti vaticani destinitari delle notifiche di atti tributari", Section II, in "Note Verbali") during a 2007 diplomatic exchange with Italy, retrieved online (21 June 2018) at: <www.vatican.va/roman_curia/secretariat_state/2015/documents/rc-seg-st-20150401_convenzione-materia-fiscale-italia-nota-verbale.pdf>. It was also annexed to a financial transparency convention signed on 1 April 2015, recorded online (retrieved 21 June 2018) at <www.vatican.va/roman_curia/secretariat_state/2015/documents/rc-seg-st-20150401_convenzione-materia-fiscale-italia_it.html>. An additional zone for Vatican Radio antennae at Santa Maria di Galeria was created by a treaty signed on 8 June 1951, and ratified in 1952; cf. "Accordo fra la Santa Sede e l'Italia per gli impianti Radio-Vaticani a Santa Maria di Galeria ed a Castel Romano", Italian Senate proceedings, retrieved online (21 June 2018) at: <www.senato.it/service/PDF/PDFServer/BGT/487741.pdf>. See also, "Zone extraterritoriali vaticani" as of 2001, Holy See website, retrieved online (21 June 2018) at: <www.vatican.va/news_services/press/documentazione/documents/sp_ss_scv/informazione_generale/extraterritoriale_it.html>; also "Lo Stato del Papa ha più territori fuori che dentro i suoi confini".

65. Cf. the Lateran Treaty, 11 February 1929, article 13, 14, and 16, and the tables in Annex 3; and the 2007 "Note Verbali", Section III.

66. Bartoloni, 119. "Declaration Recognizing the Right of Flag of States having no Sea Coast", *Convention and Statute on the Régime of Navigable Waterways of International Concern*, Barcelona, 20 April 1921.

67. At the United Nations Organization, where the Holy See is a non-member observer state, the papal flag flies under "Holy See" after the voting member states, in accordance with General Assembly resolution A/RES/69/320, "Raising the flags of non-member observer States at the United Nations", 10 September 2015. At the New York site its inaugural hoisting took place on 25 September to coincide with the visit of Pope Francis; at the Vienna site on 9 October; and at the Geneva site on 13 October. At the Organization for Security and Cooperation in Europe (Vienna) the flag flies in alphabetical order under "Saint-Siège". In the U.S. State Department lobby in Washington, the flag stands between those of Haiti and Honduras (i.e., "Holy See").

68. Cf. Holy See Press Office website, "Bilateral and Multilateral Relations of the Holy See", retrieved online (21 June 2018) at: <www.vatican.va/news_services/press/documentazione/documents/corpo-diplomatico_index_en.html>. When Vatican City is a subject of active or passive legation (which occurs rarely), its relations are handled through the Holy See's Secretariat of State (*Legge Fondamentale*, art. 2). Cf. Vatican City State website, "Participation in International Organizations", retrieved online (21 June 2018) at: <www.vaticanstate.va/content/vaticanstate/en/stato-e-governo/rapporti-internazionali/partecipazioni-ad-organizzazioni-internazionali.html>.

69. Illustration (Havana) from *Nunciatura Apostólica* en Cuba, retrieved online (24 April 2012) at: <www.nunciaturacuba.net/contacto> and (21 June 2018) at: <static.wixstatic.com/media/80fb2a08722609dac90efcaeb146c9b7.wix_mp_1024>. Illustration (Prague) from *Wikipedia*, retrieved online (21 June 2018) at: <commons.wikimedia.org/wiki/File:Praha,_apo%C5%A1tolsk%C3%A1_nunciatura,_port%C3%A1l.JPG>. Illustration (London area) from *Wimbledon News*, 7 April 2005, email and photo to author 14 December 2005; the flag was at half-staff after the death of John Paul II.

70. Reuters news photo, "A swiss guard [sic] prepares the Vatican flag before the arrival of King Mohammed VI of Morocco at the Vatican, April 13 [2000] for his meeting with Pope John Paul II", available online (23 July 2018) at: <pictures.reuters.com/archive/VATICAN-MOROCCO-RP2DRICFZLAA.html>. Also, a 2001 *National Geographic* television documentary, *Inside the Vatican*, video clip at 4:08 available online (23 July 2018) at: <www.youtube.com/watch?v=3-QbMPqFecg>.

71. *Pace* Smith, *Flags Through the Ages*, p. 223, who later acknowledged his error to this author. See photo originally published in National Geographic, December 1964 (vol. 126:6), p. 825; and available online (retrieved 1 July 2018) at: <www.gettyimages.com/detail/news-photo/king-hussein-salutes-vatican-flag-as-he-stands-next-to-pope-news-photo/80996808#/king-hussein-salutes-vatican-flag-as-he-stands-next-to-pope-paul-vi-picture-id80996808>.

72. Luigi Rangoni-Machiavelli, letter to unnamed Monsignor, 26 February 1929, in "Bandiera Pontificia", ASV, Segr. di Stato, An. 1929, Rubr. 240, fasc. 1, folio 266. Rangoni-Machiavelli proposed several flag options, including a yellow-white vertical bicolor overlaid by a centered red oval-shield, fimbriated in gold and bearing a tiara-and-keys emblem. He pointed to the papal infantry colors of the mid-1800s as precedents: see Figs. 2.11–12.

73. Illustrations from Heim, pl. V:22, and "Tributes to Pope John Paul II", *Wimbledon News*, 7 April 2005, photo (enlargement in author's archives courtesy of publisher). Cf. letter of Charles Bransom to Whitney Smith, 19 November 1980, Flag Research Center files. Heim was a papal diplomat in London from 1973 to 1985.

74. Illustration from *Legge fondamentale* (2000), annex B. Cf. Arias Pérez, pp. 31–33.

75. Alberto Serafini, 'Nota sullo stemma dello Stato Vaticano,' 1929 (undated), in "Bandiera Pontificia", ASV, Segr. di Stato, An. 1929, Rubr. 240, fasc. 1, folios 322–327. Serafini's study examined options for the state arms and recommended the design ultimately selected.

76. Cf. Fig. 1.6. To ensure visibility, heraldry requires that metals (gold and silver, or their correlates yellow and white) should only be charged upon tinctures (red, blue, green, etc.), and vice versa, unless the charge is "fimbriated" (i.e., prominently bordered) in a contrasting hue.

77. Arias Pérez, pp. 37–48. Occasionally papal embassy plaques employ the red shield anyway, including in Kenya, Sweden, and South Korea.

78. Illustration from a past version of the Holy See website (subsequently replaced by another), retrieved online (19 May 2013) at: <www.vatican.va/news_services/press/documentazione/documents/sp_ss_scv/insigne/sp_ss_scv_stemma-bandiera-sigillo_en.html> and available via <archive.org>.

79. Illustration from Holy See website, retrieved online (19 May 2013) at: <www.vatican.va/roman_curia/institutions_connected/lev/docs_lev/en/copyright_en.htm> and available via <archive.org>.

80. *Discovering the Vatican*, part 2, episode 7 ("The White Car"). "La prima papamobile", online (26 July 2018) at: <www.fcaspace.com/it/veicolo_dellaudacia_e_della_passione_sportiva_

la_prima_papamobile> and <www.fcaspace.com/media/images/papamobile/20110728_benvenuta_la_fiat_024.jpg>.

81. Ziggioto, part II, p. 101.

82. See Figures 1.26, 2.5–6, and accompanying text.

83. For example, it has been said that, when representing one or the other, the keys are juxtaposed differently on the flag. In fact, no symbolic difference attaches to the juxtaposition—as can be seen from the Vatican website, which shows the coats of arms of both entities with the gold key-handle on the dexter—and the Vatican flag, as well. The confusion may arise because the gold key-handle appears on the sinister in individual papal arms, but on the dexter in the constitutional illustrations of the Vatican flag and arms. The difference is merely a matter of custom. In actual flags, however, artistic liberty freely juxtaposes the keys, at times.

84. Illustration from *Wikipedia* author Djampa, "File: Old Jerusalem Latin Patriarch flag Vatican", photo from 1 June 2014, retrieved online (21 June 2018) at: <commons.wikimedia.org/wiki/File:Old_Jerusalem_Latin_Patriarch_flag_Vatican.jpg>.

85. Lovell: "Now that the Italian Government has recognized the State of the Vatican City (June 7, 1929), there will be two flags for the Papal States [sic]: one to be used only within the borders of the Vatican City, and the other to be used by Catholic buildings in the city of Rome.... The colors of the ... [latter] flag will be white and yellow only [i.e., without the emblem]. This flag will be displayed by buildings in Rome, which have been granted diplomatic privileges under the treaty of February 11, 1929". Cf. also Ziggioto, "Le bandiere degli stati italiani", part II, p. 100. A plain bicolor dating from circa 1950, donated to the Clarence R. Rungee Museum by a Vatican official, is now held by the Flag Heritage Foundation in Winchester, Massachusetts.

86. Bishop Bruno Bertagna, Secretary General of the Vatican City *Governatorato*, letter to Rector of Pontifical North American College in response to author's inquiry, 23 February 1993. Protocol no. 227556.

87. Walpen. Krieg. Oertle. Ales. Dreyer. Etchells.

88. Walpen, p. 110 (fresco of Guiueppe Porta in the Sala Reggia, Apostolic Palace), 112 (fresco of Nebbia and Guerra in the Salone Sistino, Apostolic Palace). Major Peter Hasler, email to author, 21 October 2006.

89. Ales, pp. 85–86, 374–375 (pl. 102), who shows a 1732 version with the nine stripes in the order of blue-yellow-red (thrice repeated) and bearing the arms of Clement XII. The 1736 painting is by Salvatore Colonelli-Sciarra, "Scenes of an Elegant Procession in the Piazza del Quirinale ..."

90. Illustrations from Pontifical Swiss Guard archives, Major Peter Hasler, email and photos to author, 28 August 2006, who states that the flag as preserved is missing a stripe. Oertle, p. 4. Piroli, ms. 71/25 (dated 1825, but showing the arms of Gregory XVI who reigned from 1831). Piroli, ms. 77/7 (1851). Piroli, ms. 78/9 (1825) & 78/14 (1850). Also, "Bandiera", watercolor number Ved10d4, held at the Istituto per la Storia del Risorgimento Italiano, Museo Centrale del Risorgimento, Sezione Iconografica, Rome. It bears the stripes in the (mistaken) order of blue-yellow-red, with the arms of Gregory XVI toward the top; at the bottom appear the arms of the Pfyffer von Altishofen family who commanded the Guards from 1712–1847. Repeated by Ales, pp. 90–91, 388–389 (pl. 109). Commanders' arms are displayed on a chart in the Swiss Guards quarters, Vatican City. Cf. roster retrieved online (21 June 2018) at <flagspot.net/flags/va-swiss.html>.

91. Illustrations from Pontifical Swiss Guard archives, Major Peter Hasler, email and photos to author, 30 March 2009.

92. Krieg, pp. 350, 447. Oertle, p. 4.

93. Illustration from Pontifical Swiss Guard archives, Major Peter Hasler, email and photo to author, 28 August 2006. Krieg, p. 447. Oertle, p. 4.

94. Illustration from Pontifical Swiss Guard archives, Major Peter Hasler, email and photo to author, 28 August 2006. Krieg, p. 447. Oertle p. 4.

95. Illustration from "Die Neue Fahne der Schweizergarde". Walpen, pp. 112, 114, pictures and explains the original sketch; also pictured online (23 July 2018) at: <www.loutan.net/olivier/archives/2016/04/13/drapeau-de-la-garde-suisse-pontificale-du-vatican/>. Oertle, p. 3. Krieg, pp. 447–448, who states that the original flag was 222 cm (87 in.) square, with the cross 32 cm (13 in.) wide.

96. The Rules state: "The flag of the Pontifical Corps of the Swiss Guards is divided by a white cross in four fields, the first of which (at the top, nearest the pole) has the coat of arms of the reigning Pope and the fourth has the arms of Julius II. Both of these are on fields of red. The second and third quarters bear the colors of the Swiss Guards that are blue, red, and yellow. At the point the arms of the cross intersect, there is the coat of arms of the Commandant in charge." Cf. Rules of the Swiss Guards, Article 3 ("The Guard—The flag", retrieved online [9 August 2010] via <www.schweizergarde.org>). The rules also state that the current flag is 2.2 m (86.6") square. Additional information on Swiss Guards flags can be found at *Flags of the World* retrieved online (21 June 2018) at <www.crwflags.com/fotw/flags/va-swiss.html>.

97. Arias Pérez, pp. 89–136.

98. Illustration from the weblog "zentral+" retrieved online (21 June 2018) at: <blogs.zentralplus.ch/de/blogs/fundstuecke/3507909/Luzerner-Wappen-im-Vatikan.htm>. Cf. "Pope Francis attends Swiss Guard flag ceremony", retrieved online (7 May 2015) at: <en.radiovaticana.va/news/2015/05/02/pope_francis_attends_swiss_guard_flag_ceremony/1141274#> and available via <archive.org>.

99. Cf. Flags of the World retrieved online (21 June 2018) at: <www.crwflags.com/fotw/flags/va-swiss.html>

100. Bruckner, pp. 164–199, shows some Julian banners. Arias Pérez, p. 91, distinguishes the modern damask patterns by time-period.

101. Illustrations from Begni, p. 11; from David, retrieved online (26 June 2018) at <www.flickr.com/photos/bigkitty/3485845272/>; and from contemporary postcard in author's archives. Krieg, p. 448, reports that before 1870 the flag flew outdoors in St. Peter's Square, near the guard-post windows inside the Bronze Doors; and afterwards, indoors only. Since 1929, it occasionally flies outdoors, but usually indoors.

102. Illustration from contemporary postcard, author's archives.

103. The *Corpo della Gendarmeria dello Stato della Città del Vaticano* received its unit flag during ceremonies honoring its patron, St. Michael the Archangel, at the Castel Gandolfo Pontifical Villa: cf. "Vatican Police Force to Join Interpol", Zenit.org, 29 September 2008; and news photo services retrieved online (9 August 2010) at <www.photo.va> and <www.catholicpress.com>. For the Gendarmerie's previous flag, see pp. 71 & 93. Cf. also online (retrieved 21 June 2018), <www.vaticanstate.va/content/vaticanstate/it/stato-e-governo/struttura-del-governatorato/corpo-della-gendarmeria.html>.

104. Illustration from postcard, "Gendarmeria Pontificia, Bandiera con scorta", Edizione "Ecclesia", ca. 1950 (arms of Pius XII), author's archives. See also Chapter 2 ("Other Flags").

105. Illustration from Francisco Gregoric, used with permission. Cordero di Montezemolo presents his original draft, p. 187f. Cf. Arias Pérez, pp. 137–140.

106. Illustration from Spink, p. 87.

107. Illustration from "Bandiera dello Stato del Vaticano a Palazzo Montecitorio in occasione della visita del Pontefice, 14 novembre 2002", *Governo Italiano, Presidenza del Consiglio dei Ministri*, retrieved online (21 June 2018) at: <presidenza.governo.it/ufficio_cerimoniale/cerimoniale/bandiere_esposizione_foto.html>.

108. "Papa: bandiera ammainata segnale che ha preceduto fine pontificato". Associated Press video archive, "Papal flag lowered as Benedict XVI's papacy ends", video available online (9 June 2018) at: <www.youtube.com/watch?v=1oLhzxlyDec>.

109. Illustration from Patrick McGuire, papal Mass at Bellahouston Park, Glasgow, 16 September 2010, retrieved online (1 July 2018) at: <www.flickr.com/photos/paddimir/5000460681/>.

110. Illustration from Sean Gallagher, "Archbishop celebrates Mass of Thanksgiving for Papal Election", Criterion Online Edition, Archdiocese of Indianapolis, 22 March 2013; retrieved online (9 June 2018) at: <www.archindy.org/criterion/local/2013/03-22/election.html>.

111. Chesterton, p. 43 (originally published in 1932): "It is part of the picturesqueness of the thing that the Papal Flag is not a devotional or delicate thing; it is a tower of crowns and a parade of keys. Above all, its white and yellow are meant for silver and gold; and that …. gold-and-silver standard of the triple crown really is in one sense an imperial flag …."

APPENDICES

Appendix I – Papal States Maritime Ensigns

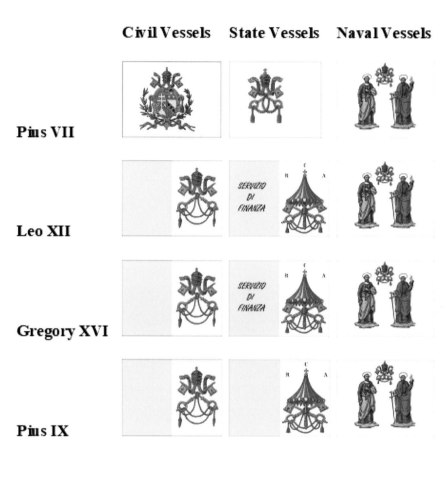

OTHER PAPAL FLAGS
(on land or in port)

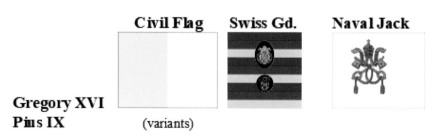

Appendix II – Papal States Military Flags

	Infantry	Civic Guard	Forts/Garrisons
Pius VII			
Leo XII			
Gregory XVI			
Pius IX Reform			
Restoration			(variants)
Mentana		**Palatine Gd.**	(variants)

Appendix III – Museum Deposits
Papal States and Related Flags

Bologna, Museo Civico del Risorgimento
- Fragment of the silk flag of the Battaglione Universitario di Bologna, 1848: 100 x 70 cm (39 x 28 in.). No. 2537. (Fig. 2.34)

Brussels, Belgium: Royal Museum of the Army
- Facsimile of the Fanion of the Tirailleurs Pontificaux Franco-Belges, Battle of Castelfidardo, 1860, held in the Historical Sala display, "Les Belges en Italie, 1860–1870": 42 x 42 cm (17 x 17 in.). (Fig. 2.18)
- Antique Photo of the framed original fanion. No. 506279.

Busset, Allier Department, France (?)
- Fanion of the Squadron Guides of General Christophe de Lamoricière, Battle of Castelfidardo, 1860, possibly held in Busset or elsewhere in Allier: 50 x 60 cm (20 x 24 in.). (Fig. 2.20)

Forlí, Italy: Museo del Risorgimento
- Civic Guard labarum, 1848: 81 cm tall x 57.5 cm long (32 in. x 23 in.), with tricolor cravat. No. 125860.

Milan, Italy: Museo del Risorgimento
- Silk flag (fort flag design), Gregory XVI: 165 x 167 cm (65 x 66 in.). Not numbered. (Fig. 1.11)

Modena, Italy: Museo Civico del Risorgimento
- Civil flag from ca. 1840 or 1850, cotton: 73 x 69 cm (29 x 27 in.). No. 795.

Nantes, France: Bertrand Malvaux Antiquities
- Zouaves tribute flag, Pius IX, 1867, silk: 125 x 103 cm (49 x 41 in.). Unknown buyer ca. 2015 (reference no. 8733). (Fig. 2.19)

Québec City, Canada: Musée de la civilization
- Distinguishing flag carried by Canadian Zouave recruits: 82 x 104 cm (32 x 41 in.). No. 1994-8507. (See p. 51)

Ravenna, Italy: Museo del Risorgimento
- "Standard" (fort flag design), Pius IX, 1847: 99 x 114 cm (39 x 45 in.). No. 237. (Fig. 1.13)

Rome: Musei Capitolini (Palazzo Senatorio, Sala delle Bandiere)
- Two Civic Guard labara from the pontificate of Pius IX: 90 x 190 cm (35 x 75 in.). No. 395–396. (Fig. 2.31)
- Fourteen Flags of the Districts of Rome (Rioni) during the pontificate of Pius IX: 176 x 176 cm (69 x 69 in.). Nos. 381-394. (cf. Fig. 2.36)

Sion (Sitten), Switzerland: Valerian Museum
- Infantry Color of the 2nd Foreign Regiment, 1846–1849: 119 x 124 cm (47 x 49 in.). No. MV 143. (cf. Fig. 2.11 discussion)

Stans, Switzerland: Nidwaldner Museum
- Infantry Color of the 2nd Foreign Regiment, 1846–1849: 117 x 126 cm (46 x 49 in.). No. NM 6863. (Fig. 2.11)

Turin, Italy: L'Armeria Reale di Torino
- Infantry Color of the 2nd Foreign Regiment, 1860: 140 x 140 cm (55 x 55 in.). No. O-23. (Fig. 2.12)

Vatican City: Museo Storico Vaticano (Lateran Palace)
- War Ensign from the warship San Pietro at surrender in 1860: 160 x 290 cm (62 x 114 in.). No. 29459. (Fig. 1.18)
- War Ensign from the corvette Immacolata Concezione, 1870: 180 x 230 cm (71 x 91 in.). No. 29458. (Fig. 1.19)
- Naval Jack (presumed) from the corvette Immacolata Concezione: ca. 120 x 180 cm (ca. 48 x 72 in.). Not displayed; unlisted in museum inventory. (Fig. 1.15)
- Civic Guard color, 1846 (157 x 163 cm [62 x 64 in.]) with cravat (32 x 283 cm [12 x 111 in.]) and staff (338 cm [133 in.]). No. 50302. (Fig. 2.30)
- Colors of the Palatine Guard from Pius IX through Paul VI. No. 30516 (Pius IX: 119 x 125 cm [47 x 49 in.]—Fig. 2.35). No. 29441 (Leo XIII). No. 29445 (Pius XI: 114 x 127 cm [45 x 50 in.]).
- Color of the Pontifical Artillery Corps under Pius IX: 100 x 90 cm (39 x 35 in.). No. 29455. (Fig. 2.37)
- Color of the Pontifical Dragoons under Pius IX: 90 x 90 cm (35 x 35 in.). No. 29456. (Fig. 2.38)
- Standard (Vessillo) of the Holy Roman Church, Noble Guard, Pius VII: 180 x 290 cm (71 x 114 in.). No. 29457. (Cf. Fig. 2.41 discussion)
- Noble Guard color, Paul VI: 90 x 90 cm (35 x 35 in.). No. 29494. (cf. Fig. 2.40 discussion)
- Fort Flag, 1870 (Castel Sant'Angelo fortress): 250 x 270 cm (98 x 106 in.). No. 30615. (Fig. 2.23)
- Flag of Prince Chigi della Rovere, Marshal of the H.R.C.

Vatican City: Gendarmerie Command
- Fort flag, 1870 (Porta Pia area fortifications): 196 x 274 cm (77 x 108 in.). Acquired 29 September 2011. (Fig. 2.21)
- Gendarmerie color, Paul VI. No. MV 54713. (cf. Fig. 3.45 discussion)

Vatican City: Swiss Guard Barracks
- Swiss Guard color, Pius IX, and likely Pius VIII & Gregory XVI: currently 216 x 228 cm (85 x 90 in.); probably originally 260 x 228 cm (102 x 90 in.). (Fig. 3.35)
- Swiss Guard color, Pius IX during Gaeta exile: 123 x 98 cm (48 x 39 in.). (Fig. 3.36)
- Swiss Guard color, Leo XIII: 280 x 270 cm (110 x 106 in.). (Fig. 3.37)
- Swiss Guard color, Pius X: 295 x 273 cm (116 x 107 in.). (Fig. 3.38)

Appendix IV – Papal States Flag "Notifications"

The following pages reproduce official Notifications from the Raccolta delle leggi e disposizioni di pubblica amministrazione nello Stato Pontificio, vol. 9 (1 January–31 December 1855), Rome: R.C.A., 1856.

Page references:
- 17 September 1825—from appendix pp. I–III (i.e., pp. 249–251)
- 8 January 1855—from pp. 1–6

APPENDICE

DELLE LEGGI E DISPOSIZIONI

RICHIAMATE NEGLI ATTI DEL PRESENTE VOLUME
PER LA PARTE TUTTORA IN VIGORE
NON RIPORTATE NEI PRECEDENTI
VOLUMI.

~~~~~

(N.1) NOTIFICAZIONE *del Camerlengato di S. R. C. sulla bandiera pontificia da inalberarsi sui legni marittimi dello Stato da commercio e da pesca.* (citata a pag. 3.)

PIER FRANCESCO *per la Misericordia di Dio*
Vescovo di Albano CARD. GALLEFFI
della S. R. C. Camerlengo

17 SETTEMBRE 1825.

Essendo la Santità di N. S. PAPA LEONE XII. felicemente regnante venuta nella determinazione di reprimere gli arbitri usati da alcuni naviganti, e di stabilire l'uniformità nei colori e nelle forme delle Bandiere pontificie, che si sogliono innalberare dai legni nello Stato, ne ha comandato di prescrivere, quanto per oracolo della stessa Santità Sua, e per l'autorità del nostro ufficio di Camerlengato veniamo ad ordinare :

1. La Bandiera pontificia, che tutti i legni dello Stato da commercio, e da pesca dovranno da qui in avanti innalberare, sarà per la metà attaccata all'asta di color giallo, e di color bianco per l'altra metà nel di cui mezzo sarà dipinto il triregno colle chiavi, a norma dei modelli depositati in tutti gli uffici di porto.

2. La Bandiera da inalberarsi dai legni addetti al servizio della Finanza sarà della stessa forma e colori, fuorichè in vece del triregno sarà dipinto nella metà bianca il gonfalone colle chiavi, sopra al quale vi saran poste le let-

— II —

tere iniziali « *Reverenda Camara Apostolica* », e nella metà di color giallo vi sarà scritto *servizio di finanza* a norma dei modelli che saranno trasmessi da Monsignor Tesoriere generale.

3. I legni mercantili dello Stato dovranno pure essere forniti di una Bandiera di riconoscimento e per chiedere soccorso, da innalberarsi sempre all'albero di maestra, la quale sarà della stessa forma e colori che la prescritta nell'art. 1. coll'aggiunta però di una fascia larga di color rosso intorno all'estremità della medesima, fuorché in quella che sta attaccata all'asta.

4. La dimensione e ampiezza di tali Bandiere saranno determinate da ciascun proprietario secondo la grandezza e portata dei legni.

5. I legni a poppa quadra, o matati a coffa l'innalbereranno sull'asta, che d'ordinario si colloca a poppa, e tutti gli altri legni l'innalbereranno sull'albero di maestra.

6. È vietato a tutti i legni sopraddetti d'innalberare sulla cima degli alberi veruna fiamma collo Stemma pontificio, ma potranno essi solamente far uso di una lunga striscia di color bianco e senza stemma.

7. In ciascun giorno festivo di precetto, ogni legno pontificio stanziato nei porti dello Stato o Esteri, sarà obbligato di tenere innalberata la suddetta Bandiera dal levare al tramontare del sole, qualora non lo impedisse un vento gagliardo e burrascoso.

8. Tutti i proprietarj de' legni da commercio saranno tenuti di fornirsi delle sopraindicate Bandiere dentro il termine di mesi quattro, e quelli de' legni da pesca dentro il termine di mesi due da computarsi dalla pubblicazione della presente notificazione.

9. Chiunque dentro il prescritto termine non avrà provveduto il suo legno delle ordinate Bandiere, o in appresso per colpevole negligenza ne mancasse, sarà punito col ritiro del passaporto marittimo.

10. Quelli poi i quali si permettessero in avvenire di cambiare in qualche modo le forme, o colori prescritti negli articoli 1. 2. 3. e 6. saranno puniti colla multa non minore di scudi dieci, e non maggiore di scudi trenta.

— III —

11. Monsig. Tesoriere generale per la parte che risguarda i legni di finanza, gl'ispettori e uffiziali di porto dello Stato, o i consoli, vice-consoli, e agenti consolari pontificj residenti no' porti esteri restano respettivamente incaricati della osservanza delle presenti disposizioni.

Data in Camera Apostolica li 17 settembre 1825.

P. F. Card. Galleffi Camerlengo di S. C.

G. Groppelli Uditore

Gioacchino M. Farinetti Segr. e Canc. della R.C.A.

———

(N.2.) *Dispaccio della Segreteria per gli affari di Stato interni N. 4689 a Monsig. Governatore di Roma sulla procedura nei giudizii economici* (citato a pag. 22).

6 settembre 1840.

La sovrana dichiarazione del 18 marzo 1838 inserita nella raccolta di quell'anno pag. 87, stabilisce per massima generale che « *allorquando si chiegga principalmente la condanna a pagare una somma a titolo di pensioni, ed in luogo di pena la espulsione del conduttore dal fondo locato, tali cause ed azioni debbano ritenersi, come cause ed azioni pecuniarie e che perciò = la competenza del giudice o tribunale si determinerà dalla somma che si richiede dall'attore,* »

Da tale massima nasce spontanea la conseguenza, che se l'azione dichiarata pecuniaria, ossia la pigione dovuta e chiesta dall'attore non supera gli scudi cinque, si fa luogo a procedere economicamente colle norme presoritte dalla sezione XXII tit. XVI part. III del moto-proprio 10 novembre 1834.

Tanto ec.

A. D. Card. Gamberini

2°

———

— 1 —

(N. 1.) *Istituzione di due nuove bandiere di distinzione d'onore da conseguirsi tanto dagli armatori di legni, quanto dai capitani della marina pontificia mercantile, oltre il premio per la costruzione de' legni nei cantieri dello Stato.*

8. gennajo 1855.

MINISTERO DEL COMMERCIO E LAVORI PUBBLICI

NOTIFICAZIONE

Fra gli oggetti che hanno sempre richiamato l'attenzione e le cure del Governo pontificio, non ultimo fu quello della marina mercantile, e volendo, per quanto è possibile, incoraggiare quelli che con la loro industria e con il loro coraggio e fatiche concorreranno all'incremento e sviluppo della marina stessa, inteso il consiglio dei Ministri, e riportatane la speciale sanzione di Sua Santità' abbiamo disposto ed ordiniamo quanto segue:

Art. 1. Saranno accordate da ora in avanti delle distinzioni onorifiche tanto agli armatori quanto ai capitani dei legni marittimi mercantili pontificii che avranno ben meritato dello Stato e del Sovrano.

Art. 2. Qualunque suddito pontificio che per proprio conto porrà in mare un materiale di mille e più tonnellate in legni marittimi

1

— 2 —

completamente attrezzati, costruiti nei cantieri dello Stato secondo la legge 10 dicembre 1825, (1) non minore ciascun legno di trecento tonnellate, avrà con questo acquistato un titolo per ottenere dal Governo pontificio un distintivo onorifico, oltre al premio di costruzione.

Art. 3. Sono istituite due bandiere o dimostrazioni d'onore, una di prima, l'altra di seconda classe, da accordarsi a quei capitani mercantili marittimi, i quali, legalmente abilitati al gran corso o al lungo corso, eseguiranno lunghi viaggi.

Art. 4. La forma delle suddette bandiere sarà la seguente.

Quella di prima classe sarà gialla e bianca contornata da una fascia rossa, con in mezzo le imagini in piedi dei Ss. apostoli Pietro e Paolo, disponendo il giallo dalla parte del ghindante.

Quella di seconda classe sarà tutta bianca contornata da una fascia gialla con in mezzo le imagini in piedi dei Ss. apostoli Pietro e Paolo.

Art. 5. Le proporzioni delle bandiere saranno ragguagliate alla grandezza e portata dei bastimenti, ma avranno per battente la misura di una volta e mezza il suo ghindante,

———

(1) Vedi vol. del 1852. parte. II. app. pag. V.

— 3 —

e la fascia che le contorna sarà larga un sesto del ghindante stesso.

Art. 6. Le suddette bandiere o dimostrazioni di onore saranno dai capitani, cui furono concesse, inalberate sul legno da essi comandato issandole, quella di prima classe in cima all'albero di maestra, e quella di seconda classe all'albero di trinchetto. Non si potrà però tenere inalberata l'una o l'altra bandiera senza che contemporaneamente sia elevata sull'asta di poppa quella dello Stato secondo la legge 17 settembre 1825. (1)

Art. 7. Per ottenere il distintivo di tali bandiere i capitani marittini sudditi pontificii dovranno provare con documenti delle rispettive autorità dello Stato, e dei rappresentanti pontificii all'estero, o in loro difetto di quelli delle potenze amiche, di avere eseguito con legni iscritti nella matricola dello Stato pontificio e debitamente approvati per il lungo e il gran corso, un dato numero di viaggi ai porti Esteri, partendo da porti pontificii con mercanzie dello Stato, e ritornandovi con mercanzie estere.

Similmente è imposto l'obbligo ai capitani marittimi che vorranno ottenere il suddetto distintivo tanto di prima che di seconda classe di tenere, specialmente per i viaggi fuori lo

1*

— 4 —

stretto di Gibilterra, un giornale meteorologico con osservazioni da farsi giornalmente alle ore quattro del mattino, al mezzodì, e alle ore otto della sera. Il Ministero del commercio, col mezzo delle magistrature di sanità e polizia de'porti in Ancona e Civitavecchia, darà gratuitamente ai capitani marittimi che imprendono tali viaggi, il modulo del giornale, con le relative istruzioni a stampa per la sua compilazione. (1) Ad ogni ritorno poi del legno al porto d'armamento, l'ufficiale del porto dovrà indilatamente ritirare l'originale del giornale stesso firmato dal capitano e dallo scrivano, onde essere subito inviato al Ministero suddetto per l'uso opportuno.

Art. 8. I porti esteri ai quali approdando possono i capitani ottenere il distintivo della bandiera sono classificati nelle seguenti quattro categorie.

1. Porti del Mar-nero.

2. Porti di Spagna, Francia, Belgio, Olanda e Inghilterra nell'Oceano, porti del Baltico, porti d'Affrica nell'Oceano fino a Capo di Buona Speranza.

3. Porti delle Americhe del Nord e del Sud nell'Oceano Atlantico, porti dell'Oceano glaciale artico.

— 5 —

4. Porti delle Indie e del grande Oceano equinoziale.

Art. 9. I distintivi delle bandiere saranno ottenuti con brevetto da rilasciarsi dal Ministero del commercio, dopo giustificati li viaggi seguenti eseguiti secondo l'art. 7.

Per ottenere quella di prima classe
   o un viaggio della quarta categoria
   o tre della terza
   o cinque della seconda.

Per ottenere quella di seconda classe
   o un viaggio della terza categoria
   o due della seconda
   o quattro della prima.

Art. 10. A quel capitano marittimo poi che avrà eseguito viaggi della terza categoria o due della quarta secondo l'art. 8, oltre alla concessione della bandiera di onore di prima classe, sarà accordato l'uso dell'uniforme d'ufficiale della marina militare pontificia col grado di tenente onorario.

Art. 11. Approdando nei porti pontificii un legno fregiato di una delle suddette due bandiere, verrà salutato dal legno guardaporto con issare la bandiera pontificia all'albero di maestra o di trinchetto a seconda della classe cui appartiene la bandiera d'onore. Se poi il capitano comandante la stessa nave fosse insignito del grado di tenente di marina, sarà inoltre salutato con tre colpi di cannone.

Art. 12. Nei casi poi di viaggi straordi-

— 6 —

narii o non contemplati di sopra, o di azioni molto onorevoli operate dai capitani, e che ridonderanno in decoro della marina e splendore della bandiera pontificia, il Governo si riserva di prendere a favore dei medesimi altre speciali disposizioni.

Art. 13. Le presenti disposizioni non potranno essere applicabili ai viaggi in corso o anteriori alla data della presente notificazione.

Art. 14. Le magistrature di sanità e polizia de'porti di Ancona, e Civitavecchia, e i sigg. rappresentanti consolari pontificii all'estero sono incaricati della esecuzione delle presenti disposizioni, ciascuno per la parte che possa loro appartenere.

Data in Roma dal Ministero del commercio e lavori pubblici li 8 gennajo 1855.

Il Ministro
G. MILESI

Segue l'istruzione

Appendix V – Vatican Flag-Flying Days

Source: Abp. Paul J. Marcinkus, President, Pontifical Commission for Vatican City State. Letter to Msgr. M. Charles Murphy in response to author's inquiry. 27 September 1983. Protocol no. 122537. (Note: for extraterritorial buildings.)

- Anniversary of pope's election
- Anniversary of the pontificate's solemn initiation
- Anniversary of the Lateran Accords (11 February)
- Pope's Name Day (i.e., his patronal feast day)
- Pope's Birthday
- Easter
- Pentecost
- Christmas
- Corpus Domini
- Solemnity of Ss. Peter & Paul (29 June)
- Public Consistories
- Beatifications
- Canonizations
- Ceremonial Opening & Closing of the Holy Door
- Anniversary of previous pope's death (half-staff)
- Papal visits to the building in question
- Papal visits into Rome in "forma ufficiale"

Source: In addition to those above, further days listed for Vatican City by Dr. Claudio Ceresa of the Vatican City Governatorate, in "Il giallo e il bianco, da due secoli colori pontifici", *L'Osservatore Romano*, 9 July 2008, p. 8.

- Solemnity of the Mother of God (1 January)
- Epiphany (6 January)
- Ascension Thursday
- Solemnity of the Assumption of Mary (15 August)
- Official State Visits to the Pope

Source: Additional days witnessed by author:

- All Saints (1 November)
- Immaculate Conception (8 December)

Appendix VI – Extraterritorial Zones of the Holy See
(Dates of notification/recognition if post-1929)

Vatican area
- Pal. S. Ufficio, Collegio Teutonico, & adjacent property
- Properties on the Janiculum Hill (multiple)
- Pal. dei Convertendi
- Pal. Pontificio Seminario [Romano] Minore (1947/1948)
- Palazzi [delle Congregazioni] ai Propilei (1959/1960)
- Pal. Pio XII (1979/1979)
- Pal. S. Paolo (via della Conciliazione 1–3; 1989/1994)
- Pal. S. Pio X (via della Conciliazione 5–7; 2002/2002)

Beyond the Vatican area
- Lateran Basilica & annexed buildings, plus the Holy Stairs
- Basilica of St. Mary Major & annexed buildings
- Basilica of St. Paul & annexed/adjacent buildings
- Pal. del Vicariato (via della Pigna)
- Pal. di Propaganda Fide
- Pal. della Cancelleria
- Pal. di S. Calisto in Trastevere

Outside Rome
- Properties in Castel Gandolfo
- Properties in S. Maria di Galeria (1951/1952)

Formerly Extraterritorial
- Pal. della Dataria (1929–1972)

Sources: "Note Verbali", Section II ("Elenco degli enti vaticani destinitari delle notifiche di atti tributari") online at: <www.vatican.va/roman_curia/secretariat_state/2015/documents/rc-seg-st-20150401_convenzione-materia-fiscale-italia-nota-verbale.pdf>; as annexed to accord with Italy, online at: <www.vatican.va/roman_curia/secretariat_state/2015/documents/rc-seg-st-20150401_convenzione-materia-fiscale-italia_it.html>. For Santa Maria di Galeria, cf. "Accordo fra la Santa Sede e l'Italia per gli impianti Radio-Vaticani a Santa Maria di Galeria ed a Castel Romano" (treaty signed on 8 June 1951, and ratified in 1952), online at: <www.senato.it/service/PDF/PDFServer/BGT/487741.pdf>. See also, "Zone extraterritoriali vaticani" as of 2001 only, Holy See website, online at: <www.vatican.va/news_services/press/documentazione/documents/sp_ss_scv/informazione_generale/extraterritoriale_it.html>. See also above, Chapter 3 ("Vatican Flag Customs").

Appendix VII – Popes Since 1800

- 1800–23   Pius VII
- 1823–29   Leo XII
- 1829–30   Pius VIII
- 1831–46   Gregory XVI
- 1846–78   Pius IX
- 1878–1903 Leo XIII
- 1903–14   Pius X
- 1914–22   Benedict XV
- 1922–39   Pius XI
- 1939–58   Pius XII
- 1958–63   John XXIII
- 1963–78   Paul VI
- 1978   John Paul I
- 1978–2005 John Paul II
- 2005–13   Benedict XVI
- 2013–   Francis

Appendix VIII – Glossary of Terms

bicolor – a flag with two stripes.

civil ensign – a flag flown from a civilian vessel, especially a merchant ship. Also, "merchant flag".

civil flag – a flag flown from a civilian establishment on land, such as a home or business.

cockade – a cloth badge, often circular, signaling political loyalties.

color – a flag carried by a military unit on foot.

cravat – strips of cloth attached near the top of a flagstaff, that hang vertically and often accompany a military color.

dexter – in heraldry, the left-hand side of a shield or emblem from the observer's point of view (i.e., the right-hand side from the shield-bearer's perspective).

ensign – in general, a flag flown ("worn") on a vessel afloat; sometimes used to describe the "war ensign" specifically.

extraterritorial – properties of the Holy See outside Vatican City that enjoy full immunity from Italian law (as do embassies). They are governed by Vatican City and fly its flag.

finial – a distinctive ornament at the top of a flagstaff.

fort flag – a flag flown by an armed garrison, such as a fort; also, "war flag". Italian: *bandiera da fortezza*.

heraldry – the design principles for coats of arms. Heraldry often informs flag design.

Holy See – the "seat" of the Catholic Church's central government (Latin, *sede* = "seat"); the papacy and its ecclesial offices. A sovereign power, it is technically distinct from its territorial state, Vatican City (see below).

infantry color – a flag carried by an infantry unit. Italian: *bandiera di guerra*.

jack – a flag worn at the bow of a vessel, usually a warship in port. Italian: *bandiera di bompresso*.

labarum – a flag-like religious banner suspended from a horizontal crossbar attached to a vertical pole, an ecclessiastical vexillum.

Lateran Accords – Three 1929 treaties which resolved a lengthy conflict between the pope and the Italian state. The "Lateran Treaty" established an independent state for the pope (Vatican City) and conferred papal recognition upon the Kingdom of Italy, in exchange for an indemnity paid to the Holy See to compensate for the loss of the Papal States. A separate "concordat" prescribed the role of the Roman Catholic Church in Italian affairs.

papal flag – a flag symbolizing papal sovereignty. Since 1929 it refers to the "Vatican flag". In the 1800s it referred to various flags representing the Papal States on land or at sea.

Papal States (also, States of the Church) – a sovereign territory administered by the pope in central Italy until 1870, when it was absorbed into Italy; in Italian, *Stato Pontificio or Stato della Chiesa.*

Piedmont – a region in northern Italy from which the campaign for Italian unification spread in the 19th century under the royal House of Savoy; officially part of the "Kingdom of Sardinia" whose capital was Turin.

pilot ensign – a flag flown by a ship to request a pilot to guide it into port. Also, "pilot jack" when flown at the bow.

Piroli Collection (*Raccolta Piroli*) – a valuable assortment of watercolors showing 19th-century Roman uniforms and flags, named for one of its many artists; preserved at the Museo Centrale del Risorgimento in Rome under its official title, *Costumi militari dello Stato Pontificio 1823–1870.*

pope – the Bishop of Rome, who succeeds St. Peter as earthly head of the Roman Catholic Church.

Risorgimento – literally, the "revival"; a movement of pan-Italian unity in the 19th century which eventually forged a unified Italian state out of the diverse states on the peninsula.

Roman Question – The question of whether the papacy or Italy should rule Rome, especially from 1870 to 1929 when the pope refused to concede the loss of the Papal States, and Italy refused to concede sovereignty to the pope.

sinister – in heraldry, the right-hand side of a shield or emblem from the observer's point of view (i.e., the left-hand side from the shield-bearer's perspective).

standard – in English (strictly speaking), a flag carried by a mounted flag-bearer. In Italian (*stendardo*), usually a flag which hangs vertically from a crossbar, or a flag with armorial bearings.

state ensign – a flag flown from a state vessel, such as a coast guard vessel.

state flag – a national flag flown on a state establishment, such as a government building.

Vatican City State – Sovereign papal territory since 1929, established by the Lateran Treaty to enshrine and protect the Holy See's independence.

vexillology – the study of flags (from *vexillum*, the Latin word for "banner").

vexillum – Latin, "flag". In English sources, a vertical banner suspended from a crossbar, attached to an upright staff. In Italian (*vessillo*) the term is more generic.

war ensign – a flag flown from a naval vessel; also "naval ensign" or simply "ensign". Italian: *bandiera da guerra or bandiera marina militare.*

war flag – see "fort flag".

Appendix IX – Flag Reconstructions

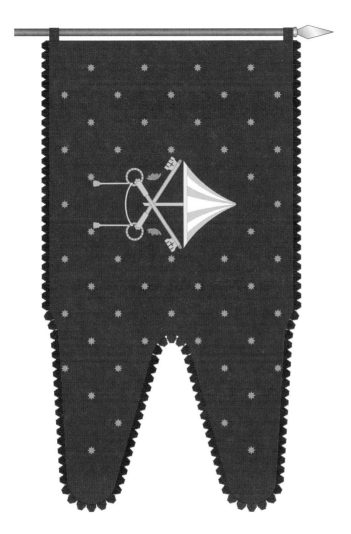

Figure 9.1. Standard of the Holy Roman Church, ca. 1930–1960 (reconstruction by Francisco Gregoric; see pp. 10, 72, 93)

Figure 9.2. Infantry color, Pius IX, with original 1846 cravat (reconstruction by Kent McDaniel; see Fig. 2.11)

Figure 9.3. Infantry color, ca. 1850–1860, Pius IX (reconstruction by Francisco Gregoric; see Fig. 2.12)

Figure 9.4. Palatine Guard color, 1859–1878, Pius IX (reconstruction by Francisco Gregoric; see Fig. 2.35)

Figure 9.5. Fort Flag variant, ca. 1849–1870; Proto-National Papal Flag, ca. 1900–1929 (reconstruction by Kent McDaniel; see Figures 2.21, 3.1–7)

Illustration Credits

Acta Apostolicae Sedis – 3.12–13. AP Photo/Claudia Gazzini – 0.1. Archives Héraldiques Suisses – 3.39. Archivio Luce – 3.8. Argo Agenzia Fotografica – 3.9. Associazione Culturale "Gaeta e il Mare" – 1.5. Author Archives – 1.7; 1.9; 1.15b; 1.18–19; 2.1; 2.8; 2.14; 2.21; 2.23–24; 2.30–31; 2.35–38; 2.42; 3.1; 3.4; 3.6–7; 3.18–19; 3.43–45; App. I–II. *Bandiere di Segnale* (Biblioteca Casanatense, Rome) – 2.2; 2.4–5. Barrett – 3.5. Begni – 3.41. Bertrand Malvaux – 2.19. Biteau – 2.20. Bruckner (Nidwalden Museum) – 2.11. Brunn-Rasmussen – 1.31. *Caras y Caretas* – 2.27. Centro Italiano Studi Vessillologici (Museo del Risorgimento di Milano) – 1.11. Charette – 2.15. Chez Hocquart – 1.6. CNS photo/Paul Haring – 0.14. Collezione Achille Rastelli – 1.20. *Courier* – 0.9. Criterion Online Edition – 3.50. Danish National Gallery – 1.30. Uli Deck/dpa via Alamy – 3.20. Fiora (L'Armeria Reale di Torino) – 2.12. Flags of the World (FOTW) – 3.30–32. Flickr.com – 0.8; 0.12; 3.17; 3.22; 3.42; 3.49. Flickr/Hernan Valencia – 0.7. Andrea Franceschini/Pacific Press via Alamy – 0.2. Gabinetto Fotografico Nazionale – 1.25. Francisco Gregoric – 2.39–40; 3.46; 9.1; 9.3–4. Heim – 3.26. *L'Illustration* – 2.22. Instagram – 0.10. Istituto per la Storia del Risorgimento Italiano (Museo Centrale del Risorgimento di Roma) – 1.28; 2.32. Istituto per la Storia del Risorgimento Italiano (Piroli) – 2.9–10; 2.28–29; 2.41. LeGras – 1.3; 1.12; 1.14; 1.17; 1.23; 2.3; 2.6. MacSwiney de Mashanaglass – 1.27. maquetland.com – 2.18. Marina Militare (Italy) – 1.15a. Kent McDaniel – 9.2; 9.5. Museo Civico Navale (Genova-Pegli) – 2.7. Museo del Risorgimento di Ravenna – 1.13. Museo Civico del Risorgimento di Bologna – 1.29; 2.33–34. Museo di Roma – 1.21; 2.25. nunciaturacuba.net – 3.23. *L'Osservatore Romano* – 0.3–6; 3.16. palazzochigi.it – 3.48. *Pavillons* – 1.8; 1.16; 1.22. Residenza Paolo VI – 0.11. *Rome in Early Photographs* (Archivio Fotografico Communale di Roma) – 2.13. Spink – 3.47. Swiss Guard Archives or websites – 1.24; 3.14–15; 3.34–38; 3.40. Underwood – 3.2. Unknown – 1.1; 0.13. Vatican Secret Archives – 3.11. vatican.va – 3.27–29. Vedo – 3.21. *Verzameling* – 1.10; 1.26; 2.26. Vigevano – 2.16; 3.10; Viviani – 2.17. Whitney Smith Flag Research Center Collection – 1.4. Wikipedia – 1.2; 3.24; 3.33. *Wimbledon News* – 3.25. Zaricor Flag Collection – 3.3.

Works Cited

Flag Manuscripts, State Archives, Official Decrees

Atti del Sommo Pontefice Pio IX, parte secondo [i.e., per lo Stato Pontificio], vol. 1. Rome: Belle Arte, 1847.

Banderas o pabellones generales de mar. 1741. Original manuscript at the Royal Palace of Aranjuez, Spain. Copy in the Whitney Smith Flag Research Center Collection archives, University of Texas at Austin.

"Bandiera Pontificia", dossier, Archivio Segreto Vaticano (ASV), *Segreteria di Stato*, Anno 1929, Rubr. 240, fascicolo 1, folios 236–330.

Bandiere di segnale delle Marine dei vari Stati. Undated 19th-century bound manuscript, ca. 1825. Copy in Biblioteca Casanatense, Rome, MS 3800 (CD-Rom CSMIN 144). Online at: <www.casanatense.it/>; <opac.casanatense.it/Record.htm?idlist=&rec ord=19917334124917355169>.

Blasone marittimo del Mediterraneo nel quale si contengono i paviglioni che si sogliono inalberare dai bastimenti delle nazioni e potenze del suo littorale e quelle delle altre nazioni e potenze fuori di esso che sogliono più frequentemente navigare in detto mare e dar fondo nel porto di Livorno. Livorno, 1765.

A Display of the Naval Flags of All Nations. London: Caxton, 1825.

Flaggen-Almanack. Hamburg: Deppermann & Ruschke, ca. 1844, pl. 15.

Flags of the World 1669–1670: A seventeenth century manuscript with commentary and historical annotations by K. L. Sierksma. Amsterdam: S. Emmering, 1966.

Galleffi, Pierfrancesco, "Notificazione", 17 September 1825 [part of B*andiere di segnale*, above; cf. also Appendix IV].

Giornale militare officiale: Anno 1866. Roma: R.C.A., 1866.

"Legge fondamentale dello Stato della Città del Vaticano": 7 June 1929, in *Acta Apostolicae Sedis – Supplemento per le leggi e disposizioni dello Stato della Città del Vaticano*, vol. 1:1 (Vatican City: Poliglotta, 8 June 1929). Revised in *Acta Apostolicae Sedis – Supplemento per le leggi e disposizioni dello Stato della Città del Vaticano*, vol. 71:18 (Vatican City: Libreria Editrice, promulgated 26 November 2000; released, 1 February 2001; reprinted, 2005).

LeGras, M. A. *Album des pavillons, guidons, flammes de toutes les puissances maritimes.* Paris: Dépôt des Cartes et Plans de la Marine, 1858, plate 22.

Maury, M. F. *Explanations and Sailing Directions to Accompany the Wind and Current Charts*, vol. 1. Washington: William A. Harris, 1858.

Milesi, Giuseppe. "Notificazione", 8 January 1855 [part of *Raccolta delle leggi*, vol. 9, below; cf. also Appendix IV].

Pagliucchi, Pio. "Bandiere pontificie di stato e militari", unpublished manuscript, 24 February 1929. Archivio Segreto Vaticano, *Segreteria di Stato*, Anno 1929, Rubr. 240, fascicolo 1, folios 269–273 (typewritten) & 279–284 (handwritten). [Part of "Bandiera Pontificia", above.]

_____. *I castellani del Castel S. Angelo.* 3 tomes. Roma: Polizzi & Valentini (vol. 1, pt. 1, 1906; vol. 1, pt. 2, 1909); and Rome: Agostiniana (vol. 2, 1928).

Pavillons des puissances maritimes en 1819. Paris, 1819, pl. 8.

Piroli, Luigi. *Costumi militari dello Stato Pontificio 1823–1870* [also known as "Piroli Collection", "Raccolta Piroli"]. Museo Centrale del Risorgimento di Roma, Library, manuscript tomes 71–79. *Parte prima dal 1823 al 1826 – 71* (vol. 1), 72 (vol. 2), 73 (vol. 3), 74 (vol. 4), 75 (vol. 5); *Parte seconda dal 1846 al 1849 – 76*; *Parte terza dal 1849 al 1870 – 77*; Appendice – 78 (vol. 1), 79 (vol. 2). Online access through tome 77 via: <www. internetculturale.it/it/>.

Quadro delle Bandiere Pontificie di Marina Militari e Mercantili. Undated flag chart (between 1855 & 1870) certified by the Secretary General of the Papal States Finance Ministry. Black-and-white photo in Whitney Smith Flag Research Center Collection archives, University of Texas at Austin; from the archives of Dr. Ottfried Neubecker (acquired from the German admiralty).

Raccolta delle leggi, decreti, ordinanze e regolamenti del governo dello Stato Romano incominciando dal 24 Novembre 1848, vol. 3. Bologna: Giuseppe Tiochhi, 1849.

*Raccolta delle leggi e disposizioni di pubblica amministrazione nello Stato Pontifici*o, vol. 2 (1 January – 15 November 1848). Rome: R.C.A., 1850.

_____, vol. 9 (1 January – 31 December 1855). Rome: R.C.A., 1856.

Regolamento della Guardia Palatina. Rome, 1859.

Rosenfeld, Friedrich Heyer von. *Die See-Flaggen, National und Provincial-Fahnen sowie Cocarden aller Laender.* Vienna: Kaiserlich-Königlichen Hof- und Staatsdruckerei, 1883, pl. 11.

Verzameling der Vlaggen by alle Natien in Gebruik [Collection of the Flags in Use by All Nations]. Amsterdam: 1844–1850. Folio on Papal States flags ("Italie. Romeinische Staat"), mostly based on a dispatch from the Netherlands ambassador in Rome dated 29 April 1834. Whitney Smith Flag Research Center Collection archives, University of Texas at Austin.

Journalistic Accounts & Eyewitness Memoirs

Il 12 Aprile 1867 a Roma: memorie dedicate alla santita di N.S. papa Pio IX felicamente regnante. Rome: *L'Osservatore Romano*, 21 June 1867.

L'Araldo della guardia nazionale e dell'esercito: Giornale militare, politico, scientifico, Naples, vol. 2:95 (24 July 1849), p. 2.

"La bandera pontificia en Buenos Aires", *Caras y caretas*, vol. 3:95 (Buenos Aires, 28 July 1900), not paginated.

Beauffort, Roger. *Histoire de l'invasion des Etats Pontificaux et du siége de Rome par l'armée italienne en Septembre 1870.* Paris: Victor Palme, 1874.

Bittard des Portes, René. *Histoire des zouaves pontificaux.* Paris: Librairie Bloud & Barral, undated [1894].

Buckingham, J. S. *France, Piedmont, Italy, Lombardy, the Tyrol, and Bavaria: An Autumnal Tour*, vol. 1. London: Peter Jackson, Late Fisher, Son, & Co., 1847.

Catalogue of Title Entries of Books and Other Articles, whole no. 651 (24 December 1903), Washington DC: Library of Congress Copyright Office, 1903.

Champagny, Franz de, et al. *Rome dans sa grandeur.* Paris: H. Charpentier, 1870, vol. 3.

Charette de la Contrie, Athanase Charles Marie, Baron de. *Souvenir du régiment des zouaves pontificaux: Rome, 1860–1870; France, 1870–1871. Notes et récits.* 2nd Edition. Paris: Alcan-Lévy, ca. 1877.

Chigi, Agostino. *Il Tempo del Papa—Re: Diario del Principe Don Agostino Chigi dall'anno 1830–1855* (2 vols.). Tolentino: Francesco Filelfo, 1906.

Civiltà Cattolica, Rome: Civiltà Cattolica, as follows:

_____, anno 11, vol. 6, 1860.

_____, anno 12, vol. 11, 1861.

_____, anno 13, vol. 2, 1862.

_____, anno 18, vol. 9, 1867.

_____, anno 18, vol. 11, 1867.

_____, anno 19, vol. 2, 1868.

_____, anno 59, vol. 2, 1908.

d'Albiousse, N. *Le fanion, le drapeau et la bannière des zouaves pontificaux.* Lille: Desclée, 1882.

"Departure of the French Troops from Rome", *The Times* [of London], 12 December 1866, p. 9a.

"The French Leave the Castle of St. Angelo", *New York Times*, 12 December 1866.

Gazzetta di Mantova, 21 July 1849 (no. 58), p. 239.

Gazzetta di Roma, 20 March 1848 (no. 46), p. 1.

Giornale di Roma. Semi-official newspaper ("Approvati e Privilegiati", 6 July 1849–19 September 1870), as noted.

"Greet Pope on Name Day", *New York Times*, 13 May 1924, p. 2.

Gregorovius, Ferdinand. *The Roman Journals of Ferdinand Gregorovius, 1852–1874*. Edited by Friedrich Althaus. Transl. A. Hamilton. London: George Bell & Sons, 1907.

Hart, Jerome. *Argonaut Letters*. San Francisco: Payot, Upham, 1901.

L'Illustrazione italiana, Rome, vol. 56:50 (15 December 1929).

"ITALY, the Papal Authority Proclaimed", New York Daily Tribune, 10 August 1849, p. 2.

"Italy and the Papacy", *The Union Review: A Magazine of Catholic Literature and Art* (London: J. T. Hayes, 1871), pp. 87–96.

Journal de Paris, 30 May 1814.

"El Jubileo de Léon XIII", *Caras y caretas*, vol. 6:235 (Buenos Aires, 4 April 1903), not paginated.

Lafort, Albert. "Le tsar Nicolas II en France (5 octobre – 9 octobre 1896)". *Revue encyclopédique. Année 1896*. Edited by Georges Moreau. Paris: Larousse, ca. 1896.

Le Chauff de Kerguenec, François [Henri]. *Souvenirs des zouaves pontificaux, 1861 et 1862* (Poitiers: Oudin, 1890).

"Liner to Fly Papal Flag: Germans Promise Protection to Archbishop on Way to Rome", *New York Times*, 17 July 1917, p. 4.

Lovell, Maj. George E., Jr. (U.S. Embassy to Italy). Letter to Colonel Robert E. Wyllis (Panama Canal Zone), 20 July 1929. Whitney Smith Flag Research Center Collection files, University of Texas at Austin.

MacFarlane, Charles. A *Glance at Revolutionized Italy: A Tour … In the Summer of 1848*, vol. 2. London: Smith, Elder, & Co., 1849.

Massimo, Principe. *Relazione del viaggio fatto da N.S. PP. Gregorio XVI alle provincie di Marittima e Campania nel maggio MDCCCXLIII*. Roma: Alessandro Monaldi, 1843.

Mathuisieulx, Henri Me?hier de. *Histoire des zouaves pontificaux*. Tours: A. Mame et fils, 1913.

Memoria que el Ministro de Estado en el despacho de relaciones exteriores presenta al congreso ordinario de 1878. Lima: Imprenta del Estado, 1878.

Il mondo illustrato: giornale universale. Turin: Giuseppe Pomba, from vol. 1 (1847) forward.

"Papa: bandiera ammainata segnale che ha preceduto fine pontificato", AGI.it, 28 February 2013. Online at: <web.archive.org/web/20130302072851/www.agi.it/cronaca/notizie/201302282044-cro-rt10307-papa_bandiera_ammainata_segnale_che_ha_preceduto_fine_pontificato>.

"The Papal Embassadors", *New York Times*, 1 August 1875, p. 12.

"Papal Flag to Fly First Time at Sea [sic]: Nuncio Going from Argentina to Belgium Charters a Ship and Carries Papal Colors", *New York Times*, 13 June 1916, p. 11.

Pesci, Ugo. *I primi anni di Roma capitale (1870–1878)*. Florence: R. Bemporad & Figlio, 1907.

Pierconti, Adriano. *Da Leone XIII a Pio X*. Rome: Cooperativa Poligrafica, 1904.

Poli, Oscar de. *Souvenirs du bataillon des Zouaves pontificaux*. Paris, Chez Tous les Libraires, 1861.

"The Pope and His Probable Future", *New York Times*, 17 December 1866, p. 4.

"Pope Announces Accord with Italy; Proclaims it Today … Pope's Election Celebrated", *New York Times*, 7 February 1929, p. 1 & 20.

"Pope Pius 67 Years Old", *New York Times*, 1 June 1924, p. E1.

"Pope Pius 72 Years Old Today", *New York Times*, 31 May 1929, p. 13.

"Pope Says Glory Will Shine Here", *New York Times*, 30 November 1911, p. 6.

"Prince Rospigliosi Dead: Papal Flag at Half Staff for Commander of the Noble Guard", *New York Times*, 7 June 1915, p. 11.

Quatrebarbes, Théodore, le Comte. *Souvenirs d'Ancone: Siége de 1860*. Paris: Charles Douniol, 1866.

"Religious Orders Exiled: Portuguese Republicans Search Papal Nuncio's Residence for Arms", *New York Times*, 9 October 1910.

"Restoration Projects", *Il Messaggero: The Newsletter of the Illinois Patrons of the Arts in the Vatican Museums*", Spring 2014, p. 1. Online at: <www.vaticanpatronschicago.org/wp-content/uploads/2015/07/PatronsNews-Spring2014.pdf>.

Revue Catholique de l'Alsace: Année 1862. Strasbourg: Louis-François le Roux, 1862.

Richards, G. B. "The Passing of a Pope and the Making of a New One", *The Historical Outlook*, vol. 13 (Philadelphia: McKinley, January–December 1922), pp. 113–118.

Roma nelle fotografie della Raccolta Ceccarius presso la Biblioteca Nazionale di Roma. Edited by Pietro Becchetti et al. Rome: Colombo, 2004.

Rome in Early Photographs: The Age of Pius IX. Photographs 1846–1878 from Roman and Danish Collections. Translated by Ann Thornton. Copenhagen: Thorvaldsen Museum, 1977.

Rouleau, Commandant C. E. *La Papauté et les zouaves pontificaux*. Québec: Le Soleil, 1905.

Semaine religieuse du Diocèse de Lyon, vol. 3:2 (29 mai 1896 – 20 novembre 1896), Lyon: Emmanuel Vitte, 1896.

Semaine religieuse du Diocèse de Lyon, vol. 10:2 (29 mai 1903 – 20 novembre 1903), Lyon: Emmanuel Vitte, 1903.

"Siége et capitulation de Città-Castellana: Seconde lettre", in *Précis historiques*, vol. 19, 1870 (Paris: E. Repos, ca. 1870), pp. 597–599.

"Soundings by Mussolini", Time, 13 February 1928. Online archive at <www.time.com>.

Special Correspondent, "The World's Modern Pilgrimage", *The Catholic World*, vol. 70:420 (March 1900), p. 773–793.

"Les troupes françaises évacuent le fort Saint-Ange, le 11 décembre. D'après un croquis de M. Zwahlen", engraving in L'Illustration: *Le Journal Universal,* vol. 48, no. 1244 (29 December 1866), p. 404. Online (7 March 2012) at: <repository.library.brown.edu/studio/item/bdr:214524>.

Willes, Lieutenant George. Letter to Vice-Admiral Sir W. Parker, 21 July 1849, aboard the *Spitfire* at Civitavecchia. *Correspondence Respecting the Affairs of Rome, 1849,* subsection p. 93 (enclosure no. 2 in entry no. 103), in *Accounts and Papers [i.e., Parliamentary Papers]*, House of Commons, United Kingdom, vol. 57 (4 February – 8 August 1851). London: HMSO, 1851.

Published Flag-Related Studies

Ales, Stefano. *Insegne militari preunitarie italiane*. Rome: Ufficio Storico dello Stato Maggiore dell'Esercito, 2001.

American Flag Company. Flag Catalog. New York & Chicago, ca. 1912.

Annin & Company. Flag Catalogs. Verona, New Jersey, 1910 & 1918.

Angst, Walter. "The Banner of the Papal Swiss Guard", *The Flag Bulletin*, vol. 38:3 (May–June 1999), p. 89–105.

Arias Pérez, Luis Miguel. *Emblemas del Estado de la Ciudad del Vaticano*. Madrid: Sociedad Española de Vexilología, 2013.

Bascapè, Giacomo C. and Marcello del Piazzo. *Insegne e simboli: araldica publica e privata medievale e moderna*. Rome: Ministero per i Beni Culturali e Ambientali, 1983.

Becker, William M. "The Adoption of the Flag of the Vatican City State, 1929", *Flagmaster*, no. 137 (December 2010), p. 10–11.

_____. "The Flag of Vatican City". Online website at <vatflag.tripod.com/>.

_____. "Flags of the Papal States: 1800–1870", *The Flag Bulletin*, vol. 42:5 (September–October 2003), p. 149–204.

_____. "The Proto-National Papal Flag", *The Flag Bulletin*, vol. 45:2 (March–April 2006), p. 42–53 plus front & back cover illustrations.

_____. "The Vatican Flag: Proportions & Alternatives", *NAVA News*, no. 213 (January–March 2012), p. 2–4.

_____. "Vatican Flags", *The Flag Bulletin*, vol. 25:6 (November–December 1986), p. 216–236.

Belardo, Mario. "Le vicende del biancogiallo", *L'Osservatore Romano*, 30 March 1956.

Brandani, Massimo, P. Crociani, and Massimo Fiorentino. *L'esercito pontificio da Castelfidardo a Porta Pia, 1860–1870: uniformi, equipaggiamento, armanento.* Milano: Intergest, 1976.

Breschi, Roberto. "Stato Pontificio", *Bandiere passato e presente*, online at: <www.rbvex.it/chiesa.html>.

Bruckner, A. & B. *Schweizer Fahnenbuch.* St. Gallen: Zollikofer, 1942.

Catalogo degli oggetti esposti nel padiglione del Risorgimento Italiano: Esposizione Generale Italiana di Torino, 1884. Milano: Fratelli Dumolard, 1888.

Ceresa, Claudio. "Il giallo e il bianco, da due secoli colori pontifici", *L'Osservatore Romano*, 9 July 2008, p. 8. Translated as "Vatican City State Flag Flies for Two Centuries", *L'Osservatore Romano: Weekly Edition in English*, 6 August 2008, p. 12.

Colangeli, Oronzo. *Simboli e bandiere nella storia del risorgimento italiano.* Bologna: Pàtron, 1965.

Cordero Lanza di Montezemolo, Andrea, and Antonio Pompili. *Manuale di Araldica Ecclesiastica nella Chiesa Cattolica.* Vatican City: Librería Editrice Vaticana, 2014.

"Les couleurs pontificales", *Le Franc Tireur* (Brussels), vol. 44:17 (22 April 1909), p. 2.

Crociani, P. "Le truppe pontificie di riserva e le loro uniformi (1803–1870)", *Armi Antiche* (Turin: Accademia di S. Marciano, 1973), p. 389–437.

Defontaine, Henri. "Le bataillon des tirailleurs franco-belges: Bataille de Castelfidardo—18 sept. 1860". *Le Passepoil*, vol. 7:3 (1927), p. 33–39 & pl. 4.

"Drapeaux pontificaux", *Annuaire Pontifical Catholique.* Edited by Msgr. Albert Battandier. Paris: Bonne Presse, 1909, p. 95–102.

Dreyer, Emil. "Flags of the Pope's Swiss Guard since 1798". Proceedings of the 22nd International Congress of Vexillology, Berlin, 2007, p. 427–471. Online via <http://internationalcongressesofvexillology-proceedingsandreports.yolasite.com/>.

Erdmann, Carl. *Das Wappen und die Fahne der Römischen Kirche.* Rome: W. Regenberg, 1931.

Etchells, Arthur William III. "The Swiss Guard of the Popes – flags and uniforms and their inter-relations: The early period 1506–1806". Proceedings of the 22nd International Congress of Vexillology, Berlin, 2007, p. 399–426. Online via <http://internationalcongressesofvexillology-proceedingsandreports.yolasite.com/>.

Fedeltà palatina: stampato a cura del Comando della Guardia palatina d'onore di Sua Santità. Rome: A. Belardetti, 1945.

Ferrari, G. "Bandiere italiane ..." *Dizionario del risorgimento nazionale*, vol. 1, p. 83–84. Edited by Michele Rosi. Milan: Francesco Vallardi, 1931.

Fiora, Paolo Edoardo. *Bandiere in Piemonte.* Turin: Accademia di S. Marciano, 1971.

Galbreath, Donald Lindsay. *Papal Heraldry.* Edited by Geoffrey Briggs. London: Heraldry Today, 1972.

Ghisi, Enrico. *Il Tricolore Italiano 1796–1870.* Milan: Rizzoli, 1931.

Governatorato dello Stato della Città del Vaticano. 1929–2009: *Ottanta anni dello Stato della Città del Vaticano.* Vatican City: Biblioteca Apostolica Vaticana, 2009.

Grand Larousse Illustré du XXe siècle. 1929.

Heim, Bruno B. *Heraldry in the Catholic Church.* Humanities: Atlantic Highlands, NJ, 1978.

Holy See Press Office. "Storia della bandiera dello Stato della Città del Vaticano." From *Mondo vaticano. Passato e presente*. Edited by Niccolò Del Re. Vatican City: Libreria Editrice Vaticana, 1995. Online at: <www.vatican.va/news_services/press/documentazione/documents/sp_ss_scv/insigne/bandiera_storia_it.html>.

Krieg, Paul M. *Die Schweizergarde in Rom*. Lucerne: Räber & CIE, 1960, p. 446–449.

Lancellotti, Arturo. "La corte pontificia. La Guardia Nobile", *Emporium* 69:411 (Bergamo, 1929), p. 143–159, available online at: <www.artivisive.sns.it/fototeca/scheda.php?id=41998>.

_____. *Mondo vaticano. Storia aneddottica della città vaticana*. Milan: Athena, 1930.

MacSwiney de Mashanaglass, Valentine Emmanuel Patrick, Marchese . *La coccarda pontificia. Appunti storici*. Roma: Tipographia Vaticana, 1908.

Martin, Jules, de Montalbo, and Raymond Richebe. *Armoires et decorations*. Paris: Librairie des Contemporains, 1896.

"Die neue Fahne der Schweizergarde", *Archives Héraldiques Suisses / Schweizerisches Archiv für Heraldik*, vol. 28: 4 (Zürich: Imprimérie Schulthess & Co., 1914), pp. 205–206 & Plate 5.

Oertle, Vincenz. "'… aux couleurs du pape régnant' – Die Fahne der Päpstlichen Schweizergarde", *Zeitschrift für Heereskunde*, no. 419 (January/March 2006), pp. 1–6.

Panetta, Rinaldo. "Im Ziechen Petri: Die Staatsflagge des Vatikans", *Osservatore della Domenica*, 11 March 1979.

Pidoux, Sir P. A. "Le drapeau pontifical", *Rivista del Collegio Araldico [Rivista Araldica]*, vol. 9:6 (Rome, 1911), pp. 343–346.

_____. "Les origines de la cocarde pontificale", *Rivista del Collegio Araldico [Rivista Araldica]*, vol. 7 (Rome, 1909), pp. 429–440.

Rangoni-Machiavelli, Luigi. "Bandiera", *Enciclopedia italiana di scienze, lettere ed arti*, vol. 6, pp. 74–80. Rome: Istituto Giovanni Treccani, 1938.

Roma 1846–1849: dalle riforme di Pio IX alla Repubblica Romana. Edited by the Assessorato alla Cultura, Comune di Roma. Rome: Multigrafica, 1987. Commemorative booklet, Museo del Folklore exhibition, Rome, 9 February to 15 March 1987.

Smith, Whitney. *The Flag Book of the United States*. New York: William Morrow, 1975.

_____. *Flags Through the Ages & Across the World*. New York: McGraw-Hill, 1974.

Usai, Michelangelo (ed.). *La Guardia Palatina d'onore di Sua Santità*. Rome: Industrie Grafiche L. Coluzza, 1942.

Van Dijk, S. J. P. "Banner", *New Catholic Encyclopedia*, vol. 2, pp. 51–52. New York: McGraw-Hill, 1967.

Vigevano, Colonel Attilio. *La fine dell'esercito pontificio*. Rome: Stabilimento Poligrafico per l'Amministrazione della Guerra, 1920.

Viviani, Camillo. *L'esercito pontificio in alta uniforme negli ultimi anni prima del 1870*. Bergamo: Ist. Ital. D'Arti Grafiche, 1918; multilingual, plates 7 & 9.

Walpen, Robert. *La Guardia Svizzera Pontificia. Acriter et fideliter*. Coraggio e fedeltà. 2nd edition. Locarno, Switzerland: Armando Dadò, 2005, pp. 110–114.

Wise, Terrance. *Military Flags of the World*. New York: Arco, 1977.

Zara, Luigi. "La bandiera pontificia", *Rivista del Collegio Araldico [Rivista Araldica]*, vol. 27 (Rome, 1929), pp. 134–137.

Ziggioto, Aldo. "La bandiera della marina pontificia di finanza", Il Finanziere vol. 86:10 (May 31, 1972), pp. 21–22.

_____. "Le bandiere degli stati italiani (Parte I)", *Armi Antiche* (Torino: Accademia di S. Marciano, 1981), pp. 91–124. "Le bandiere degli stati italiani (Parte II)", *Armi Antiche* (Torino: Accademia di S. Marciano, 1982), pp. 97–102.

"Les Zouaves pontificaux du Canada: le drapeau des zouaves canadiens", *L'album universel*, vol. 22, no. 1130 (16 December 1905), p. 1031. Online image (no. 6909) provided by

Bibliothèque et Archives Nationales du Québec at: <bibnum2.banq.qc.ca/bna/illustrations/htm/d2006.htm>.

Supplemental Resources

"Agostino Rivarola" [papal legate of Pius VII], Wikipedia, retrieved online at: <it.wikipedia.org/wiki/Agostino_Rivarola>.

Alvarez, David. *The Pope's Soldiers*. Lawrence: Kansas University Press, 2011.

Andreotti, Giulio & Giovanni Spadolini. "Il giorno più lungo di Roma capitale: Il centenario della breccia di Porta Pia", special insert in edition titled "I cento anni di Porta Pia", *Domenica del Corriere*, 11 August 1970.

Andrieux, Maurice. *Daily Life in Papal Rome in the Eighteenth Century*. London: George Allen & Unwin, 1968.

Artaud de Montor, Alexis François. *Histoire du Pape Pie VII*, vol. 2. Paris: Adrien le Clere, 1839.

Barrett, William E. Shepherd of Mankind: A Biography of Pope Paul VI. Garden City: Doubleday, 1964.

Bartoloni, Bruno. "Here's the Vatican", *Ulisse 2000* (Alitalia flight magazine), October–November 1985.

Begni, Ernesto. *The Vatican: Its History – Its Treasures*. New York: Letters & Arts, 1914.

Biteau, Jérôme. "Les volontaires pontificaux à cheval ou guides de La Moricière (1860) – Espoir et fidélité", in *La Sabretache et la Plume*, undated research publication, online at: <lasabretache.fr/wp-content/uploads/2017/08/Les-volontaires-pontificaux-%C3%A0-cheval.pdf>.

Blasi, Benedetto. *Del danno che avverrebbe allo Stato Pontificio da qualunque strada ferrata di communicazione fra la Toscana e l'Adratico*. Rome: Belle Arti, 1846.

Bonetti, A. M. *Pio IX ad Imola e Roma*. Naples: A. e Salv. Festa, 1892.

Bouquet, M. "The Papal Navy and its English Ships", *The Dublin Review*, vol. 23 (July 1938), pp. 62–77.

Capefigue, Jean-Baptiste-Honoré-Raymond. *L'Europe pendant le consulat et l'empire de Napoléon*, vol. 12. Brussels: Société Belge de Librairie, 1841.

Cesare, Raffaele de. *The Last Days of Papal Rome*. New York: Houghton Mifflin, 1909.

Chesterton, G .K. "Christendom in Dublin", *The Collected Works of G.K. Chesterton*, vol. 20, pp. 35–81. San Francisco: Ignatius, 2001.

Corona, Germano (Ed.) . "Genova e Don Orione: Un amore a prima vista", *Amici di Don Orione*, Genoa, vol. 40:6 (October 2001), unpaginated. Reprinted as "Progetto Don Orione: Approfondimento", *Fondazioneinforma*, 9:2 (May–August 2007), p. 14. Online at: <www.donorione-genova.it/genova-e-don-orione/introduzione/>.

Coulombe, Charles A. *The Pope's Legion: The Multinational Fighting Force that Defended the Vatican*. New York: Palgrave MacMillan, 2008.

Denis-Delacour, Christopher. "Flying the Pope's Flag", *Quaderni Storici* vol. 48:2 (August 2013), pp. 395–417.

Discovering the Vatican [Alla Scoperta del Vaticano]. DVD. Produced by Przemys?aw Häuser and Krzysztof Masztalerz. Telewizja Polska S.A., 2006.

Donovan, Jeremiah. *Rome Ancient and Modern*, vol. 3. Rome: Crispino Puccinelli, 1843.

Gasbarri, Carlo, et al. *Strenna dei Romanisti*. Rome: Staderini, 1953.

Guide to the Vatican Museums. Edited by the Monumenti, Musei e Gallerie Pontificie. Florence: Conti Tipicolor, 1979.

Hoffmann, Paola. *Le ville di Roma e dei dintorni*. Rome: Newton & Compton, 2001.

Innocenti, Lorenzo. *Per il papa re: Il risorgimento Italiano visto attraverso la storia del Reggimento degli Zuavi Pontifici, 1860/1870* (Perugia: Esperia, 2004).

L'Italia nei cento anni del secolo XIX (Milan: Antonio Vallardi, 1900–03; sequential pages across multiple volumes).

Kertzer, David. *The Pope who would be King*. New York: Random House, 2018.

_____. *Prisoner of the Vatican*. Boston: Houghton Mifflin, 2004.

Lafond, Edmond. Rome, *lettres d'un pèlerin*, vol. 2. Paris: Ambroise Bray, 1856.

Macadam, Alta (ed.). *Blue Guide to Rome and Environs*. New York: Rand McNally, 1979.

Madelin, Louis. *La Rome de Napoléon*. Paris: Plon-Nourrit, 1906.

Marden, Luis. "The Other Side of Jordan", *National Geographic* 126:6 (December 1964), pp. 790–825.

Marraro, Howard R. "Canadian and American Zouaves in the Papal Army, 1868–1870". CCHA Report 12 (1944–45): 83–102. Online at: <www.umanitoba.ca/colleges/st_pauls/ccha/Back%20Issues/CCHA1944-45/Marraro.pdf>.

Martina, Giacomo. *Pio IX (1846–1850). Miscellanea Historiae Pontificiae*, vol. 38. Rome: Gregorian University, 1974.

"New Fundamental Law Promulgated for Vatican City State", *L'Osservatore Romano: Weekly Edition in English*, 14 February 2001, p. 5. Online at: <www.ewtn.com/library/CHIS-TORY/VATCNLAW.HTM>.

"Note Verbali", diplomatic exchange between the Holy See and Italy, 20 July 2007, online at: <www.vatican.va/roman_curia/secretariat_state/2015/documents/rc-seg-st-20150401_convenzione-materia-fiscale-italia-nota-verbale.pdf>; as referenced at <www.vatican.va/roman_curia/secretariat_state/2015/documents/rc-seg-st-20150401_convenzione-materia-fiscale-italia_it.html>.

Nouaille-Degorce, Patrick. Mentana, with Laurent Gruaz, *L'Attentat de la caserne Serristori*. Allaire: Éditions Edilys, 2017.

O'Clery, The [Patrick Keyes]. *The Making of Italy*. London: Kegan Paul, Trench, Trübner & Co., 1892.

Pinto, Michelangelo. *Don Pirlone a Roma: Memorie di un Italiano dal 1 settembre 1848 al 31 dicembre 1850*. Turin: Progresso, 1853 (3 volumes combined).

Pizzuti, Mario. *Guardia di Finanza, 1975* [Calendar]. *Cenni sulla Marina di Finanza Pontificia*. Milan: Commando Generale della Guardia di Finanza, unpaginated.

Savio, Oscar. "I cimeli del 20 Settembre: a Porta Pia – la fanfara dei Bersaglieri", *Storia illustrata*, Settembre 1970 (no. 154, "20 Settembre 1870 – la presa di Roma"), pp. 52–63.

Scott, James Brown. *Cases on International Law*. St. Paul, Minnesota: West, 1922.

Spink, Kathryn. *John Paul II: In the Service of Love*. New York: Mayflower, 1979.

"Lo Stato del Papa ha più territori fuori che dentro i suoi confini." *Il Messaggero*, 10 January 1994, p. 20.

Tabet, Guido. *L'Italia nel 1848–49*. Milan: Alfieri & LaCroix, 1923?

Williamson, Benedict. *The Treaty of the Lateran*. London: Burns, Oates & Washbourne Ltd., 1929.

n.b.: Online references above were current as of 22 June 2018.

About the Author

Rev. William M. Becker is a Roman Catholic priest of the Diocese of Winona-Rochester (Minnesota, USA). After undergraduate studies at St. Mary's University of Minnesota, he studied theology at the Pontifical Gregorian University in Rome, completing a doctorate (S.T.D.) in 1994. Ordained in 1988, he has served in parish, chancery, seminary, and academic roles. He is currently a pastor in Plainview, Minnesota. Flags have interested him since boyhood; he joined NAVA in 1977. He specializes in flags of his native Minnesota, as well as the papacy, having lived in Rome for eight years. His vexillological work has appeared in the *Flag Bulletin*, *NAVA News*, *Minnesota History*, *Flagmaster*, and now *Raven*.

Colophon

This issue of *Raven: A Journal of Vexillology* was typeset in Adobe Garamond Pro using Adobe InDesign CS3. Typesetting and image processing was performed by Jeanne E. Galick Graphic Design, Portland, Oregon. The cover design was based on concepts developed by Douglas Lynch. The text generally follows the *Chicago Manual of Style*, except to adopt the more-logical British conventions regarding punctuating around quoted material.

This journal is printed on 70-pound matte coated text paper. Printing and binding was done by Signature Book Printing, www.sbpbooks.com.